Purchased 10-22-'85
Tuesday
At Lincoln Birthday
Cabin Feb 12, 1809.
This small Cabin, is inclosed
in a Sand Stone Building,
A Shrine, that all Men,
and Women should see "

THE FACE OF
LINCOLN

THE FACE OF
LINCOLN

Compiled and Edited by
JAMES MELLON

BONANZA BOOKS
NEW YORK

Manufactured in the United States of America

Library of Congress Cataloging in Publication Data

The Face of Lincoln.

"Photographic poses...(accompanied by)
Lincoln's written and spoken words, interspersed with eyewitness descriptions of the
man"—Introd.
1. Lincoln, Abraham, 1809–1865—Portraits.
I. Mellon, James.
E457.6.F33   1982   973.7′092′4   82-4297
                                                AACR2

ISBN: 0-517-383330

h g f e d c b

For my father,
Matthew Taylor Mellon,
with affection and gratitude

Lincoln's features were the despair of every artist who undertook his portrait. The writer saw nearly a dozen, one after another, soon after the first nomination to the presidency, attempt the task. They put into their pictures the large rugged features, and strong prominent lines; they made measurements to obtain exact proportions; they 'petrified' some single look, but the picture remained hard and cold. Even before these paintings were finished it was plain to see that they were unsatisfactory to the artists themselves, and much more so to the intimate friends of the man; this was not he who smiled, spoke, laughed, charmed. The picture was to the man as the grain of sand to the mountain, as the dead to the living. Graphic art was powerless before a face that moved through a thousand delicate gradations of line and contour, light and shade, sparkle of the eye and curve of the lip, in the long gamut of expression from grave to gay, and back again from the rollicking jollity of laughter to that serious, faraway look that with prophetic intuitions beheld the awful panorama of war, and heard the cry of oppression and suffering. There are many pictures of Lincoln; there is no portrait of him.

John Nicolay,
Secretary to President Lincoln

In the year 1862, with the nation sundered but with the forces gathering that would one day make it whole again, Nathaniel Hawthorne undertook to interview the President of the United States for *The Atlantic Monthly*.

"President Lincoln," he came to write, "is the essential representative of all Yankees, and the veritable specimen, physically, of what the world seems determined to regard as our characteristic qualities." Indeed, it was this general representativeness, at least as much as his distinction, that millions of Lincoln's countrymen had responded to.

As the noted Lincoln scholar Professor J. G. Randall observed, "The Americanism of the man is revealed with an effect that is almost startling if one looks at the full standing form . . . and then tries to imagine that figure in court costume, with knee-breeches, close fitting stockings, and buckles. There was little of Europe here. . . . The man's appearance was both unique and related to a well known American type, the type that might have been found among people close to the woods or mountains."

Today, as in Lincoln's time, America is described, almost ceremonially, as a melting pot of nationalities. Yet, from this speculative diversity a national character has evolved. Certain values and attitudes are acknowledged as "American"; likewise, certain faces in the crowd are recognized at once as American faces—that is, faces which America alone has made possible.

In Lincoln's face, as in the story of his life, every American can see something made of this country's toil, something atavistic, for Lincoln remains the nonpareil example of the American character as it forged, and sought to define, itself. It must be fiercely lonely to be on such terms with history.

The extreme conditions of Lincoln's presidency, his preternatural ability to master these conditions, and the agonized night he was torn away from the nation in his height and glory have all served to nourish the Lincoln myth, in which the man himself, the creature of flesh and blood, has been so long imprisoned.

The machinery of hagiography has been at work a hundred years and more. To the slaves, Lincoln was "the Great Messiah"; in

Deteriorating original glass collodion negative made by
Anthony Berger at Mathew Brady's gallery, in Washington, D.C., February 9, 1864.
Reproduced from an enlarged positive printed on film.
Library of Congress.

Overleaf, left and right: *Broken original glass collodion negatives made*
by Alexander Hesler, in Springfield, Illinois, June 3, 1860.
Reproduced from gelatin silver prints.
Smithsonian Institution.

the popular press, he was "Honest Abe" and "the Railsplitter." After his assassination, he landed at once in the country of the saints: artists painted him with wings sprouting from his shoulders, flying up to heaven to be kissed on the forehead by Washington. There, too, on the rim of sainthood, Walt Whitman placed him, "the sweetest, wisest soul of all my days and lands." And Civil War veterans who had worn the blue and had risked all to save "the last, best hope of earth" would continue to speak of him as "the President," because for them there could never be another. But stirring beneath these glittering badges was a man.

The present generation has dealt less deferentially with traditional heroes. The value of self-reliance, individualism, free enterprise, and advancement through hard work—American virtues all—is now openly debated. As old institutions crumble and new ones come into view, it is not surprising that Lincoln, who embodied older virtues, should be the victim of historical revisionism. But the consequences are not what his detractors imagine. In punishing him for having been apotheosized, they have refused him the right to be a man—proving nothing so much as their own failure to recognize that with Lincoln the seeds of the myth *were* largely in the man. He would have been a restless and unsatisfactory saint. He was a complicated and little-knowable man, to whom life was a great trouble but who had learned how to stand with life. The man has been diminished before and has recovered, restored to the myth.

Though there is no such thing as a completely objective book, *The Face of Lincoln* is at least innocent of biographical pretensions.

It does not claim to portray the one and only Lincoln. Still, whoever wishes to know him must at some point take a look at him, and this book concentrates on photographs of Lincoln's face. It is a face at times strangely unaware of itself, revealing an inner as well as an outer dimension, a face now shockingly human in its dilapidation, now comic in its lack of symmetry, sometimes the very embodiment of holiness—a face whose masks at once beckon and forbid.

Lincoln took care to spice the frequent remarks he made about his homeliness with just enough humor to leave listeners in doubt as to his true opinion. It is a fact that he was a not unwilling visitor to photographic galleries, that he enjoyed inscribing photographs of himself to friends, and that, once in the White House, he became America's first widely photographed president.

At least 136 photographic poses or views of Lincoln are believed to have existed. Among the 120 that survive, either in original form or as copies, are daguerreotypes (images on silver-plated copper), tintypes, also known as ferrotypes (images on japanned iron), ambrotypes (glass collodion negatives converted into positives by the addition of a dark background), various sizes of gold-toned images, including stereographic cards and cartes-de-visite, all printed on albumen paper from glass collodion negatives, and a few salt prints and glass positives, also printed from collodion negatives. *The Face of Lincoln* exists to preserve in their finest possible form these monuments of photography—the last surviving glimpses of the greatest of all Americans.

The sad and low condition of most Lincoln photographs has

lent this project a particular urgency. Many of the photographs have been desecrated or destroyed. Many more have been stolen, most flagrantly from public institutions easy of access. The fugitive nature of the photographic chemicals themselves has caused many of the original albumen prints to fade, often into indistinctness.

Of the 103 surviving poses known, or believed, to have originated as glass collodion negatives made for printing, there are only 24 for which an original, or suspected original, negative can still be found. The remaining seventy-eight poses survive only as original prints or as copies of lost originals. All but a few of the remaining original negatives are severely scratched, cracked, or broken, or suffer from deteriorating emulsion. Of the fourteen existing poses known, or believed, to have originated as ambrotypes, only four survive in the original. Of the two known original daguerreotypes, one survives. And at least sixteen poses of Lincoln are believed to have existed, of which not a single likeness remains.

Locating, and obtaining permission to reproduce, the best surviving likeness of each Lincoln pose was a formidable challenge. Hundreds of prints in dozens of private and public collections across America had to be compared. Invaluable originals, many of them signed by Lincoln, had to be transported to the printer so that reproductions could be made directly from them, rather than from copies, to which previous compilers had resorted. On four separate occasions, Richard Benson, the most accomplished printer of historical glass negatives, was prevailed upon to come to Washington, D.C., to print film positives from the original negatives in the Library of Congress, the National Archives, and the Smithsonian Institution.

By printing enlarged positives on a special film rather than on paper, the printer has been able to extract from the original glass negatives entire areas of Lincoln's face that appear washed out in the traditional paper prints. The images preserved in these glass negatives are in many cases reproduced here for the first time in all their richness of detail. Where there were two or more likenesses of the same pose, the one revealing the greater amount of lifelike skin surface in Lincoln's face was reproduced. Discarded were those likenesses where the complexion is largely whitened out, so that Lincoln appears distant and impersonal, as though in a lithograph—where, although we are looking at him, we never have the feeling that he is looking at us. Lincoln is, after all, a transcendental figure to Americans—a veritable god of the hearth. It amounts almost to sacrilege that photographs of him exist. But something of the god in him must yield when in a photograph we can reach out and touch him, reduced to his true human size, a figure suddenly released from historic time, as full of the future as of the past.

In these photographs, Lincoln's expression is normally serious, if not downright somber. There are a number of reasons for this: In Lincoln's time, photographic exposures were so lengthy that if the subject did not remain motionless at a sitting and hold his facial expression while the camera was open, his photographic image would become blurred. Also, Lincoln, who loathed affectations, would have felt awkward holding a smile for several seconds. A smiling Lincoln would have been awkward in any case, for contrived grinning in photographs had not yet become obligatory, let alone reached epidemic proportions. Finally, Lincoln was a somber man by disposition. He was capable of breaking into helpless laughter, of humor and bonhomie, but mirth was the minor key of his nature. Even under a smile, the melancholy remained; it "seemed to roll from his shoulders and drip from the ends of his fingers," one of his contemporaries intoned.

With the exception of one early daguerreotype, all the known photographic poses of Lincoln were made during the last eleven years of his life—between 1854, when he was forty-five years old, and 1865. By a fortunate coincidence, these were the years of Lincoln's prominence—when he spoke much, and wrote much, that would record the metamorphosis of the lawyer-politician into the embattled Civil War president.

The text of this book consists of Lincoln's written and spoken words, interspersed with eyewitness descriptions of the man. And this is as it should be: we need no trumpets to proclaim him, no supporting piers, when Lincoln's very words are the bridge from him to us.

His face, which is not the least of his monuments, also tells his story. Grappling with the mutinous, intractable issues of slavery and secession, at war with his own prejudices, unable, in any case, to abandon his actions, which had imperiled the nation and might yet destroy it, as he searched he aged beyond calendar and clock. Of the pile of years there were to be only fifty-six, and yet the face continues to bear witness, as if it were itself the conclusion of the whole unsparing world.

James Mellon

A broken frame of the original multiple-image
stereographic negative made by Alexander Gardner, in Washington, D.C., August 9, 1863.
Reproduced from an enlarged positive printed on film. Brown University.

THE FACE OF
LINCOLN

As I would not be a *slave*,
so I would not be a *master*.
This expresses my idea of democracy—
Whatever differs from this,
to the extent of the difference,
is no democracy—

Private meditation.

1

Lincoln Introduces Himself:
Sketch for a Campaign Biography

J. W. Fell, Esq   Springfield,
My dear Sir: Dec. 20. 1859

Herewith is a little sketch, as you requested. There is not much of it, for the reason, I suppose, that there is not much of me. . . .

I was born Feb. 12, 1809, in Hardin County, Kentucky. My parents were both born in Virginia, of undistinguished families—second families, perhaps I should say. My mother, who died in my tenth year, was of a family of the name of Hanks, some of whom now reside in Adams, and others in Macon counties, Illinois. My paternal grandfather, Abraham Lincoln, emigrated from Rockingham County, Virginia, to Kentucky, about 1781 or 2, where, a year or two later, he was killed by indians, not in battle, but by stealth, when he was laboring to open a farm in the forest. His ancestors, who were quakers, went to Virginia from Berks County, Pennsylvania. An effort to identify them with the New-England family of the same name ended in nothing more definite, than a similarity of Christian names in both families, such as Enoch, Levi, Mordecai, Solomon, Abraham, and the like.

My father, at the death of his father, was but six years of age; and he grew up, literally without education. He removed from Kentucky to what is now Spencer county, Indiana, in my eighth year. We reached our new home about the time the State came into the Union. It was a wild region, with many bears and other wild animals still in the woods. There I grew up. There were some schools, so called; but no qualification was ever required of a teacher, beyond *"readin, writin, and cipherin,"* to the Rule of Three. If a straggler supposed to understand latin, happened to sojourn in the neighborhood, he was looked upon as a wizzard. There was absolutely nothing to excite ambition for education. Of course when I came of age I did not know much. Still somehow, I could read, write, and cipher to the Rule of Three; but that was all. I have not been to school since. The little advance I now have upon this store of education, I have picked up from time to time under the pressure of necessity.

I was raised to farm work, which I continued till I was twenty two. At twenty one I came to Illinois, and passed the first year in Illinois—Macon county. Then I got to New-Salem (at that time in Sangamon, now in Menard county), where I remained a year as a sort of Clerk in a store. Then came the Black-Hawk war; and I was elected a Captain of Volunteers—a success which gave me more pleasure than any I have had since. I went the campaign, was elated, ran for the Legislature the same year (1832) and was beaten—the only time I have been beaten by the people. The next, and three succeeding biennial elections, I was elected to the Legislature. I was not a candidate afterwards. During this Legislative period I had studied law, and removed to Springfield to practice it. In 1846 I was once elected to the lower House of Congress. Was not a candidate for re-election. From 1849 to 1854, both inclusive, practiced law more assiduously than ever before. Always a whig in politics, and generally on the whig electoral tickets, making active canvasses. I was losing interest in politics, when the repeal of the Missouri Compromise aroused me again. What I have done since then is pretty well known.

If any personal description of me is thought desirable, it may be said, I am, in height, six feet, four inches, nearly; lean in flesh, weighing, on an average, one hundred and eighty pounds; dark complexion, with coarse black hair, and grey eyes—no other marks or brands recollected. Yours very truly

A. LINCOLN

Lincoln's earliest known photographic likeness, made probably in 1846,
when at the age of thirty-seven he was elected to the U.S. House of Representatives.
Original daguerreotype, believed to have been made by N. H. Shepherd,
in Springfield, Illinois. Library of Congress.

2

The Frontier Lawyer; Notes for a Law Lecture

I am not an accomplished lawyer. I find quite as much material for a lecture in those points wherein I have failed, as in those wherein I have been moderately successful. The leading rule for the lawyer, as for the man of every other calling, is diligence. Leave nothing for to-morrow which can be done to-day. Never let your correspondence fall behind. Whatever piece of business you have in hand, before stopping, do all the labor pertaining to it which can then be done. When you bring a common-law suit, if you have the facts for doing so, write the declaration at once. If a law point be involved, examine the books, and note the authority you rely on upon the declaration itself, where you are sure to find it when wanted. The same of defenses and pleas. In business not likely to be litigated,—ordinary collection cases, foreclosures, partitions, and the like,—make all examinations of titles, and note them, and even draft orders and decrees in advance. This course has a triple advantage; it avoids omissions and neglect, saves your labor when once done, performs the labor out of court when you have leisure, rather than in court when you have not. Extemporaneous speaking should be practised and cultivated. It is the lawyer's avenue to the public. However able and faithful he may be in other respects, people are slow to bring him business if he cannot make a speech. And yet there is not a more fatal error to young lawyers than relying too much on speech-making. If any one, upon his rare powers of speaking, shall claim an exemption from the drudgery of the law, his case is a failure in advance.

Discourage litigation. Persuade your neighbors to compromise whenever you can. Point out to them how the nominal winner is often a real loser—in fees, expenses, and waste of time. As a peacemaker the lawyer has a superior opportunity of being a good man. There will still be business enough.

Never stir up litigation. A worse man can scarcely be found than one who does this. Who can be more nearly a fiend than he who habitually overhauls the register of deeds in search of defects in titles, whereon to stir up strife, and put money in his pocket? A moral tone ought to be infused into the profession which should drive such men out of it.

The matter of fees is important, far beyond the mere question of bread and butter involved. Properly attended to, fuller justice is done to both lawyer and client. An exorbitant fee should never be claimed. As a general rule never take your whole fee in advance, nor any more than a small retainer. When fully paid beforehand, you are more than a common mortal if you can feel the same interest in the case, as if something was still in prospect for you, as well as for your client. And when you lack interest in the case the job will very likely lack skill and diligence in the performance. Settle the amount of fee and take a note in advance. Then you will feel that you are working for something, and you are sure to do your work faithfully and well. Never sell a fee note—at least not before the consideration service is performed. It leads to negligence and dishonesty—negligence by losing interest in the case, and dishonesty in refusing to refund when you have allowed the consideration to fail.

There is a vague popular belief that lawyers are necessarily dishonest. I say vague, because when we consider to what extent confidence and honors are reposed in and conferred upon lawyers by the people, it appears improbable that their impression of dishonesty is very distinct and vivid. Yet the impression is common, almost universal. Let no young man choosing the law for a calling for a moment yield to the popular belief—resolve to be honest at all events; and if in your own judgment you cannot be an honest lawyer, resolve to be honest without being a lawyer. Choose some other occupation, rather than one in the choosing of which you do, in advance, consent to be a knave.

Fragment, undated, probably written during the 1850s

Lincoln at the age of forty-five.
Gelatin silver print of a lost contemporary print
of the lost presumed daguerreotype made in Chicago
by Johan Carl Frederic Polycarpus Von Schneidau, in 1854.
Courtesy of George Rinhart.

3

On Slavery

This *declared* indifference, but as I must think, covert *real* zeal for the spread of slavery, I can not but hate. I hate it because of the monstrous injustice of slavery itself. I hate it because it deprives our republican example of its just influence in the world—enables the enemies of free institutions, with plausibility, to taunt us as hypocrites—causes the real friends of freedom to doubt our sincerity, and especially because it forces so many really good men amongst ourselves into an open war with the very fundamental principles of civil liberty—criticising the Declaration of Independence, and insisting that there is no right principle of action but *self-interest*. . . .

Before proceeding, let me say I think I have no prejudice against the Southern people. They are just what we would be in their situation. If slavery did not now exist amongst them, they would not introduce it. If it did now exist amongst us, we should not instantly give it up. This I believe of the masses north and south. Doubtless there are individuals, on both sides, who would not hold slaves under any circumstances; and others who would gladly introduce slavery anew, if it were out of existence. We know that some southern men do free their slaves, go north, and become tip-top abolitionists; while some northern ones go south, and become most cruel slave-masters.

When southern people tell us they are no more responsible for the origin of slavery, than we, I acknowledge the fact. When it is said that the institution exists, and that it is very difficult to get rid of it, in any satisfactory way, I can understand and appreciate the saying. I surely will not blame them for not doing what I should not know how to do myself. If all earthly power were given me, I should not know what to do, as to the existing institution. My first impulse would be to free all the slaves, and send them to Liberia,—to their own native land. But a moment's reflection would convince me, that whatever of high hope, (as I think there is) there may be in this, in the long run, its sudden execution is impossible. If they were all landed there in a day, they would all perish in the next ten days; and there are not surplus shipping and surplus money enough in the world to carry them there in many times ten days. What then? Free them all, and keep them among us as underlings? Is it quite certain that this betters their condition? I think I would not hold one in slavery, at any rate; yet the point is not clear enough for me to denounce people upon. What next? Free them, and make them politically and socially, our equals? My own feelings will not admit of this; and if mine would, we well know that those of the great mass of white people will not. Whether this feeling accords with justice and sound judgment, is not the sole question, if indeed, it is any part of it. A universal feeling, whether well or ill-founded, can not be safely disregarded. We can not, then, make them equals. It does seem to me that systems of gradual emancipation might be adopted; but for their tardiness in this, I will not undertake to judge our brethren of the south.

From a speech at Peoria, Illinois, October 16, 1854

"The picture . . . is, I think, a very true one;
though my wife, and many others, do not. My impression is that their objection
arises from the disordered condition of the hair," wrote Lincoln of this
pose, made when he was forty-eight. Contemporary varnished albumen print from the
lost original negative made by Alexander Hesler, in Chicago,
February 28, 1857. Ostendorf Collection.

4

*Two Fragments on the Equality of Men and
the Declaration of Independence*

I think the authors of that notable instrument [the Declaration of Independence] intended to include *all* men, but they did not intend to declare all men equal *in all respects*. They did not mean to say all were equal in color, size, intellect, moral developments, or social capacity. They defined with tolerable distinctness, in what respects they did consider all men created equal—equal in "certain inalienable rights, among which are life, liberty, and the pursuit of happiness." This they said, and this meant. They did not mean to assert the obvious untruth, that all were then actually enjoying that equality, nor yet, that they were about to confer it immediately upon them. In fact they had no power to confer such a boon. They meant simply to declare the *right*, so that the *enforcement* of it might follow as fast as circumstances should permit. They meant to set up a standard maxim for free society, which should be familiar to all, and revered by all; constantly looked to, constantly labored for, and even though never perfectly attained, constantly approximated, and thereby constantly spreading and deepening its influence, and augmenting the happiness and value of life to all people of all colors everywhere. The assertion that "all men are created equal" was of no practical use in effecting our separation from Great Britain; and it was placed in the Declaration, not for that, but for future use. Its authors meant it to be, thank God, it is now proving itself, a stumbling block to those who in after times might seek to turn a free people back into the hateful paths of despotism. They knew the proneness of prosperity to breed tyrants, and they meant when such should re-appear in this fair land and commence their vocation they should find left for them at least one hard nut to crack.

From a speech at Springfield, Illinois, June 26, 1857

The Savior, I suppose, did not expect that any human creature could be perfect as the Father in Heaven; but He said, "As your Father in Heaven is perfect, be ye also perfect." He set that up as a standard, and he who did most towards reaching that standard, attained the highest degree of moral perfection. So I say in relation to the principle that all men are created equal, let it be as nearly reached as we can. If we cannot give freedom to every creature, let us do nothing that will impose slavery upon any other creature.

From a speech at Chicago, July 10, 1858

*Ambrotype copy of the lost original ambrotype
made by Amon J. T. Joslin, in Danville, Illinois, probably during
late April or May of 1857 or 1858, when Lincoln was attending court
in Vermilion County. Ostendorf Collection.*

5

Lincoln's Challenge
to the Incumbent Senator from Illinois, Stephen A. Douglas

. . . Judge Douglas is especially horrified at the thought of the mixing [of] blood by the white and black races: agreed for once—a thousand times agreed. There are white men enough to marry all the white women, and black men enough to marry all the black women; and so let them be married. On this point we fully agree with the Judge; and when he shall show that his policy is better adapted to prevent amalgamation than ours we shall drop ours, and adopt his. Let us see. In 1850 there were in the United States, 405,751, mulattoes. Very few of these are the offspring of whites and *free* blacks; nearly all have sprung from black *slaves* and white masters. A separation of the races is the only perfect preventive of amalgamation but as an immediate separation is impossible the next best thing is to *keep* them apart *where* they are not already together. If white and black people never get together in Kansas, they will never mix blood in Kansas. That is at least one self-evident truth. A few free colored persons may get into the free States, in any event; but their number is too insignificant to amount to much in the way of mixing blood. In 1850 there were in the free states, 56,649 mulattoes; but for the most part they were not born there—they came from the slave States, ready made up. In the same year the slave States had 348,874 mulattoes all of home production. The proportion of free mulattoes to free blacks —the only colored classes in the free states—is much greater in the slave than in the free states. It is worthy of note too, that among the free states those which make the colored man the nearest to equal the white, have, proportionably the fewest mulattoes, the least of amalgamation. In New Hampshire, the State which goes farthest towards equality between the races, there are just 184 Mulattoes while there are in Virginia—how many do you think? 79,775, being 23,126 more than in all the free States together.

These statistics show that slavery is the greatest source of amalgamation, and next to it, not the elevation, but the degeneration of the free blacks. Yet Judge Douglas dreads the slightest restraints on the spread of slavery, and the slightest human recognition of the negro, as tending horribly to amalgamation.

From a speech at Springfield, Illinois, June 26, 1857

Allow me now, in my own way, to state with what aims and objects I did enter upon this campaign. I claim no extraordinary exemption from personal ambition. That I like preferment as well as the average of men may be admitted. But I protest I have not entered upon this hard contest solely, or even chiefly, for a mere personal object. I clearly see, as I think, a powerful plot to make slavery universal and perpetual in this nation. The effort to carry that plot through will be persistent and long continued, extending far beyond the senatorial term for which Judge Douglas and I are just now struggling. I enter upon the contest to contribute my humble and temporary mite in opposition to that effort.

Fragment: Notes for speeches, August 21, 1858

Albumen print of the lost ambrotype made by Samuel G. Alschuler,
in Urbana, Illinois, April 25, 1858. Mellon Collection.

6

If we could first know *where* we are, and *whither* we are tending, we could then better judge *what* to do, and *how* to do it.

We are now far into the *fifth* year, since a policy was initiated, with the *avowed* object, and *confident* promise, of putting an end to slavery agitation.

Under the operation of that policy, that agitation has not only, *not ceased*, but has *constantly augmented*.

In *my* opinion, it *will* not cease, until a *crisis* shall have been reached, and passed.

"A house divided against itself cannot stand."

I believe this government cannot endure, permanently half *slave* and half *free*.

I do not expect the Union to be *dissolved*—I do not expect the house to *fall*—but I *do* expect it will cease to be divided.

It will become *all* one thing, or *all* the other.

Either the *opponents* of slavery, will arrest the further spread of it, and place it where the public mind shall rest in the belief that it is in course of ultimate extinction; or its *advocates* will push it forward, till it shall become alike lawful in *all* the States, *old* as well as *new*—*North* as well as *South*.

Opening remarks of the "House Divided Speech,"
at Springfield, Illinois, June 16, 1858

Here Lincoln is still wearing the suit he wore in court
several hours earlier when his most celebrated case ended triumphantly
with the acquittal of sixteen-year-old Duff Armstrong of premeditated murder.
Original ambrotype made by Abraham Byers, in Beardstown, Illinois,
May 7, 1858. University of Nebraska.

7

*His Law Partner William Herndon's Recollections
of Lincoln as an Orator*

. . . When he rose to speak to the jury or to crowds of people he stood inclined forward—was awkward—angular—ungainly—odd . . . ; he was a diffident man, somewhat, and a sensitive one, and both of these added to his oddity—awkwardness . . . as it seemed to me. Lincoln had confidence, full and complete confidence in himself. . . . Lincoln's voice was, when he first began speaking, shrill—squeaking—piping—unpleasant: his general look—his form—his pose—the color of his flesh wrinkled and dry, his sensitiveness & his momentary diffidence, everything seemed to be against him, but he soon recovered. I can see him now—in my mind distinct. On rising to address the jury or the crowd he . . . generally placed his hands behind him, the back part of his left hand resting in the palm of his right hand. As he proceeded and grew warmer he moved his hands to the front of his person, generally interlocking his fingers and running one thumb around the other. Sometimes his hands, for a short while, would hang by his side. In still growing warmer as he proceeded in his address he used his hands—especially and generally his right hand in his gestures: He used his head a great deal in speaking, throwing or jerking or moving it now here and now there—now in this position and now in that, in order to be more emphatic—to drive the idea home. Mr. Lincoln never beat the air—never sawed space with his hands—never acted for stage effect—was cool—calm, earnest—sincere—truthful—fair—self possessed—not insulting—not dictatorial—was pleasing—good natured, had great strong naturalness of look, pose, and act—was clear in his ideas—simple in his words—strong, terse and demonstrative: he spoke and acted to convince individuals and masses: he used . . . his right hand, sometimes shooting out that long bony forefinger of his to dot an idea or to enforce a thought, resting his thumb on his middle finger. Bear in mind that he did not gesticulate much and *yet* . . . every organ of his body was in motion and acted with ease—elegance and grace—so it all looked *to me*.

As Mr. Lincoln proceeded further . . . , if time—place—subject and occasion admitted of it, he . . . gradually warmed up—his shrill—squeaking—piping voice became harmonious, melodious—musical, . . . with face . . . aglow: his form dilated—swelled out and he rose up a splendid form, erect straight and dignified: he stood square on his feet with both legs up and down, toe even with toe—. . . He kept his feet parallel and . . . not far from each other. When Mr. Lincoln rose up to speak, he rose slowly—steadily—firmly: he never moved much about on the stand or platform when speaking, touching no desk—table—railing: he ran his eyes slowly over the crowd, giving them time to be at ease and to completely recover himself. . . . He frequently took hold with his left hand, his left thumb erect, of the left lapel of his coat, keeping his right hand free to gesture in order to . . . clinch an idea. In his greatest inspiration he held both of his hands out above his head at an angle of about fifty degrees—hands open or clinched according to his feelings and his ideas. If he was moved in some indignant and half mad moment against slavery or wrong . . . and seemed to want to tear it down—trample it beneath his feet and to eternally crush it, then he would extend his arms out, at about the above . . . angle with clinched big, bony, strong hands on them—. If he was defending the right—if he was defending liberty—eulogizing the Declaration of Independence, then he extended out his arms—palms of his hands upward somewhat at about the above degree—angle, as if appealing to some superior power for assistance and support; or that he might embrace the spirit of that which he so dearly loved. It was at such moments that he seemed inspired, fresh from the hands of his creator. Lincoln's gray eyes would flash fire when speaking against slavery or spoke volumes of hope and love when speaking of Liberty—justice and the progress of mankind—

William Herndon, in a letter to Truman Bartlett,
July 19, 1887

*Lincoln, at the age of forty-nine, the day before he clashed with
Senator Stephen A. Douglas, at Freeport, Illinois,
in the second Lincoln-Douglas debate.
Solio print of the lost ambrotype made by T. P. Pearson, in Macomb, Illinois,
August 26, 1858. Mellon Collection.*

Overleaf, left: *Gelatin silver print of a lost carbon enlargement
of the lost ambrotype believed to have been made by Preston Butler, in Springfield,
Illinois, during the summer of 1858. Meserve Collection.*
Right: *Gelatin silver print of a lost probable ambrotype
made by an unknown photographer, probably in Illinois, about 1858.*
Mellon Collection.

Yours truly
A. Lincoln.

8

On the Declaration of Independence and
Its Application to the Negro

My declarations upon this subject of negro slavery may be misrepresented, but can not be misunderstood. I have said that I do not understand the Declaration to mean that all men were created equal in all respects. They are not our equal in color; but I suppose that it does mean to declare that all men are equal in some respects; they are equal in their right to "life, liberty, and the pursuit of happiness." Certainly the negro is not our equal in color—perhaps not in many other respects; still, in the right to put into his mouth the bread that his own hands have earned, he is the equal of every other man, white or black. In pointing out that more has been given you, you can not be justified in taking away the little which has been given him. All I ask for the negro is that if you do not like him, let him alone. If God gave him but little, that little let him enjoy.

When our Government was established, we had the institution of slavery among us. We were in a certain sense compelled to tolerate its existence. It was a sort of necessity. We had gone through our struggle and secured our own independence. The framers of the Constitution found the institution of slavery amongst their other institutions at the time. They found that by an effort to eradicate it, they might lose much of what they had already gained. They were obliged to bow to the necessity. They gave power to Congress to abolish the slave trade at the end of twenty years. They also prohibited it in the Territories where it did not exist. They did what they could and yielded to the necessity for the rest. I also yield to all which follows from that necessity. What I would most desire would be the separation of the white and black races.

From a speech at Springfield, Illinois, July 17, 1858

The Declaration of Independence was formed by the representatives of American liberty from thirteen States. . . . These communities, by their representatives in old Independence Hall, said to the whole world of men: "We hold these truths to be self evident: that all men are created equal; that they are endowed by their Creator with certain unalienable rights; that among these are life, liberty and the pursuit of happiness." This was their majestic interpretation of the economy of the Universe. This was their lofty, and wise, and noble understanding of the justice of the Creator to His creatures. [Applause.] Yes, gentlemen, to *all* His creatures, to the whole great family of man. In their enlightened belief, nothing stamped with the Divine image and likeness was sent into the world to be trodden on, and degraded, and imbruted by its fellows. They grasped not only the whole race of man then living, but they reached forward and seized upon the farthest posterity. They erected a beacon to guide their children and their children's children, and the countless myriads who should inhabit the earth in other ages. Wise statesmen as they were, they knew the tendency of prosperity to breed tyrants, and so they established these great self-evident truths, that when in the distant future some man, some faction, some interest, should set up the doctrine that none but rich men, or none but white men, were entitled to life, liberty and the pursuit of happiness, their posterity might look up again to the Declaration of Independence and take courage to renew the battle which their fathers began—so that truth, and justice, and mercy, and all the humane and Christian virtues might not be extinguished from the land; so that no man would hereafter dare to limit and circumscribe the great principles on which the temple of liberty was being built. [Loud cheers.]

From a speech at Lewistown, Illinois, August 17, 1858

*Contemporary albumen print from the lost original negative
believed to have been made by Roderick M. Cole, in Peoria, Illinois,
about 1858.* Courtesy of Donald Gibson.

9

"This Is the Whole of It"

Now gentlemen, I don't want to read at any greater length, but this is the true complexion of all I have ever said in regard to the institution of slavery and the black race. This is the whole of it, and anything that argues me into his [Douglas's] idea of perfect social and political equality with the negro*, is but a specious and fantastic arrangement of words, by which a man can prove a horse chestnut to be a chestnut horse. [Laughter.] I will say here, while upon this subject, that I have no purpose directly or indirectly to interfere with the institution of slavery in the States where it exists. I believe I have no lawful right to do so, and I have no inclination to do so. I have no purpose to introduce political and social equality between the white and the black races. There is a physical difference between the two, which in my judgment will probably forever forbid their living together upon the footing of perfect equality, and inasmuch as it becomes a necessity that there must be a difference, I, as well as Judge Douglas, am in favor of the race to which I belong, having the superior position. I have never said anything to the contrary, but I hold that notwithstanding all this, there is no reason in the world why the negro is not entitled to all the natural rights enumerated in the Declaration of Independence, the right to life, liberty and the pursuit of happiness. [Loud cheers.] I hold that he is as much entitled to these as the white man. I agree with Judge Douglas he is not my equal in many respects—certainly not in color, perhaps not in moral or intellectual endowment. But in the right to eat the bread, without leave of anybody else, which his own hand earns, *he is my equal and the equal of Judge Douglas, and the equal of every living man.* [Great applause.]

*In the Lincoln-Douglas debates, Douglas repeatedly accused Lincoln of favoring equality between the white and black races.

From the first Lincoln-Douglas debate, at Ottawa, Illinois,
August 21, 1858

[Lincoln] was swarthy as an Indian, with wiry, jet-black hair, which was usually in an unkempt condition. He wore no beard, and his face was almost grotesquely square, with high cheek bones. His eyes were bright, keen, and a luminous gray color, though his eyebrows were black like his hair. His figure was gaunt, slender and slightly bent. He was clad in a rusty-black Prince Albert coat with somewhat abbreviated sleeves. His black trousers, too, were so short that they gave an appearance of exaggerated size to his feet. He wore a high stove-pipe hat, somewhat the worse for wear, and he carried a gray woolen shawl. . . .

The journalist Martin Rindlaub,
after watching Lincoln debate Douglas

Solio print of a lost likeness of unknown kind made by an unknown photographer, probably in Illinois about 1858. Mellon Collection.

10

Lincoln Characterizes Senator Douglas

There is still another disadvantage under which we labor, and to which I will ask your attention. It arises out of the relative positions of the two persons who stand before the State as candidates for the Senate. Senator Douglas is of world wide renown. All the anxious politicians of his party, or who have been of his party for years past, have been looking upon him as certainly, at no distant day, to be the President of the United States. They have seen in his round, jolly, fruitful face, postoffices, landoffices, marshalships, and cabinet appointments, chargeships and foreign missions, bursting and sprouting out in wonderful exuberance ready to be laid hold of by their greedy hands. [Great laughter.] And as they have been gazing upon this attractive picture so long, they cannot, in the little distraction that has taken place in the party, bring themselves to give up the charming hope; but with greedier anxiety they rush about him, sustain him, and give him marches, triumphal entries, and receptions beyond what even in the days of his highest prosperity they could have brought about in his favor. On the contrary nobody has ever expected me to be President. In my poor, lean, lank face, nobody has ever seen that any cabbages were sprouting out. [Tremendous cheering and laughter.] These are disadvantages all, taken together, that the Republicans labor under. *We* have to fight this battle upon principle, and upon principle alone.

From a speech at Springfield, Illinois, July 17, 1858

Gelatin silver print of a lost retouched print of the lost
original ambrotype made by William Judkins Thomson, in Monmouth, Illinois,
October 11, 1858. Mellon Collection.

11

Senator Douglas Makes Some Personal Remarks about His Opponent

In the remarks I have made on this platform, and the position of Mr. Lincoln upon it, I mean nothing personally disrespectful or unkind to that gentleman. I have known him for nearly twenty-five years. There were many points of sympathy between us when we first got acquainted. We were both comparatively boys, and both struggling with poverty in a strange land. I was a school-teacher in the town of Winchester, and he a flourishing grocery-keeper in the town of Salem. [Applause and laughter.] He was more successful in his occupation than I was in mine, and hence more fortunate in this world's goods. Lincoln is one of those peculiar men who perform with admirable skill everything which they undertake. I made as good a school-teacher as I could and when a cabinet maker I made a good bedstead and tables, although my old boss said I succeeded better with bureaus and secretaries than anything else; [cheers] but I believe that Lincoln was always more successful in business than I, for his business enabled him to get into the Legislature. I met him there, however, and had a sympathy with him, because of the up hill struggle we both had in life. He was then just as good at telling an anecdote as now. ["No doubt."] He could beat any of the boys wrestling, or running a foot race, in pitching quoits or tossing a copper, could ruin more liquor than all the boys of the town together [uproarious laughter], and the dignity and impartiality with which he presided at a horse race or fist fight, excited the admiration and won the praise of everybody that was present and participated. [Renewed laughter.] I sympathised with him, because he was struggling with difficulties and so was I. Mr. Lincoln served with me in the Legislature in 1836, when we both retired, and he subsided, or became submerged, and he was lost sight of as a public man for some years. In 1846, when Wilmot introduced his celebrated proviso, and the Abolition tornado swept over the country, Lincoln again turned up as a member of Congress from the Sangamon district. I was then in the Senate of the United States, and was glad to welcome my old friend and companion. Whilst in Congress, he distinguished himself by his opposition to the Mexican war, taking the side of the common enemy against his own country; ["That's true."] and when he returned home he found that the indignation of the people followed him everywhere, and he was again submerged or obliged to retire into private life, forgotten by his former friends. ["And will be again."] He came up again in 1854, just in time to make this Abolition or Black Republican platform, in company with Giddings, Lovejoy, Chase, and Fred Douglass for the Republican party to stand upon.

Senator Stephen A. Douglas, in the first
Lincoln-Douglas debate, at Ottawa, Illinois,
August 21, 1858

Quarter-plate daguerreotype of the lost original,
almost certainly an ambrotype or daguerreotype, believed to have been made
by Christopher S. German, in Springfield, Illinois,
during late September 1858. Courtesy of Larry West.

Yours truly
A. Lincoln.

12

On Racial Equality

While I was at the hotel to-day an elderly gentleman called upon me to know whether I was really in favor of producing a perfect equality between the negroes and white people. [Great laughter.] While I had not proposed to myself on this occasion to say much on that subject, yet as the question was asked me I thought I would occupy perhaps five minutes in saying something in regard to it. I will say then that I am not, nor ever have been in favor of bringing about in any way the social and political equality of the white and black races, [applause]—that I am not nor ever have been in favor of making voters or jurors of negroes, nor of qualifying them to hold office, nor to intermarry with white people; and I will say in addition to this that there is a physical difference between the white and black races which I believe will for ever forbid the two races living together on terms of social and political equality. And inasmuch as they cannot so live, while they do remain together there must be the position of superior and inferior, and I as much as any other man am in favor of having the superior position assigned to the white race. I say upon this occasion I do not perceive that because the white man is to have the superior position the negro should be denied everything. I do not understand that because I do not want a negro woman for a slave I must necessarily want her for a wife. [Cheers and laughter.] My understanding is that I can just let her alone. I am now in my fiftieth year, and I certainly never have had a black woman for either a slave or a wife. So it seems to me quite possible for us to get along without making either slaves or wives of negroes. I will add to this that I have never seen to my knowledge a man, woman or child who was in favor of producing a perfect equality, social and political, between negroes and white men. . . . I will also add to the remarks I have made (for I am not going to enter at large upon this subject) that I have never had the least apprehension that I or my friends would marry negroes if there was no law to keep them from it, [laughter] but as Judge Douglas and his friends seem to be in great apprehension that they might, if there were no law to keep them from it, [roars of laughter] I give him the most solemn pledge that I will to the very last stand by the law of this State, which forbids the marrying of white people with negroes. [Continued laughter and applause.] I will add one further word, which is this, that I do not understand there is any place where an alteration of the social and political relations of the negro and the white man can be made except in the State Legislature—not in the Congress of the United States—and as I do not really apprehend the approach of any such thing myself, and as Judge Douglas seems to be in constant horror that some such danger is rapidly approaching, I propose as the best means to prevent it that the Judge be kept at home and placed in the State Legislature to fight the measure. [Uproarious laughter and applause.]

Lincoln's opening statement in the fourth Lincoln-Douglas debate,
at Charleston, Illinois, September 18, 1858

13

On the Principle of Slavery

Suppose it is true, that the negro is inferior to the white, in the gifts of nature; is it not the exact reverse justice that the white should, for that reason, take from the negro, any part of the little which has been given him? *"Give* to him that is needy" is the christian rule of charity; but "Take from him that is needy" is the rule of slavery.

The sum of pro-slavery theology seems to be this: "Slavery is not universally *right*, nor yet universally *wrong*; it is better for *some* people to be slaves; and, in such cases, it is the Will of God that they be such."

Certainly there is no contending against the Will of God; but still there is some difficulty in ascertaining, and applying it, to particular cases. For instance we will suppose the Rev. Dr. Ross has a slave named Sambo, and the question is "Is it the Will of God that Sambo shall remain a slave, or be set free?" The Almighty gives no audible answer to the question, and his revelation—the Bible—gives none—or, at most, none but such as admits of a squabble, as to its meaning. No one thinks of asking Sambo's opinion on it. So, at last, it comes to this, that *Dr. Ross* is to decide the question. And while he considers it, he sits in the shade, with gloves on his hands, and subsists on the bread that Sambo is earning in the burning sun. If he decides that God wills Sambo to continue a slave, he thereby retains his own comfortable position; but if he decides that God wills Sambo to be free, he thereby has to walk out of the shade, throw off his gloves, and delve for his own bread. Will Dr. Ross be actuated by that perfect impartiality, which has ever been considered most favorable to correct decisions?

But, slavery is good for some people!!! As a *good* thing, slavery is strikingly peculiar, in this, that it is the only good thing which no man ever seeks the good of, *for himself*.

Nonsense! Wolves devouring lambs, not because it is good for their own greedy maws, but because it is good for the lambs!!!

Fragment, undated, probably about October 1, 1858

That is the real issue. That is the issue that will continue in this country when these poor tongues of Judge Douglas and myself shall be silent. It is the eternal struggle between these two principles—right and wrong—throughout the world. They are the two principles that have stood face to face from the beginning of time; and will ever continue to struggle. The one is the common right of humanity and the other the divine right of kings. It is the same principle in whatever shape it develops itself. It is the same spirit that says, "You work and toil and earn bread, and I'll eat it." [Loud applause.] No matter in what shape it comes, whether from the mouth of a king who seeks to bestride the people of his own nation and live by the fruit of their labor, or from one race of men as an apology for enslaving another race, it is the same tyrannical principle.

From Lincoln's concluding remarks in the final Lincoln-Douglas debate,
at Alton, Illinois, October 15, 1858

Lincoln at the age of forty-nine.
Gelatin silver print of the original ambrotype
made by Calvin Jackson, in Pittsfield, Illinois, October 1, 1858,
and presented by Lincoln to his friend and fellow lawyer Colonel Dick Gilmer,
of Pittsfield. Mellon Collection.

14

After Losing to Douglas in the Senate Race of 1858

Anson Miller, Esq.   Springfield,
My dear Sir   Nov. 19, 1858
    Your very kind and complimentary letter of the 15th. was received yesterday; and for which I sincerely thank you. In the last canvass I strove to do my whole duty both to our cause, and to the kind friends who had assigned me the post of honor; and now if those friends find no cause to regret that they did not assign that post to other hands, I have none for having made the effort, even though it has ended in personal defeat. I hope and believe seed has been sown that will yet produce fruit. The fight must go on. Douglas managed to be supported both as the best means to *break down*, and to *uphold* the slave power. No ingenuity can long keep those opposing elements in harmony. Another explosion will come before a great while. Yours very truly

A. Lincoln

Dr. A. G. Henry   Springfield, Ills. Nov. 19, 1858
My dear Sir
    . . . You doubtless have seen, ere this, the result of the election here. Of course I *wished*, but I did not much *expect* a better result. The popular vote of the State is with us . . .
    I am glad I made the late race. It gave me a hearing on the great and durable question of the age, which I could have had in no other way; and though I now sink out of view, and shall be forgotten, I believe I have made some marks which will tell for the cause of civil liberty long after I am gone. . . .

Autograph letter, unsigned

And by the successful, and the unsuccessful, let it be remembered, that while occasions like the present bring their sober and durable benefits, the exultations and mortifications of them are but temporary; that the victor shall soon be the vanquished, if he relax in his exertion; and that the vanquished this year may be victor the next, in spite of all competition.
    It is said an Eastern monarch once charged his wise men to invent him a sentence, to be ever in view, and which should be true and appropriate in all times and situations. They presented him the words: *"And this, too, shall pass away."* How much it expresses! How chastening in the hour of pride!—how consoling in the depths of affliction! "And this, too, shall pass away." And yet let us hope it is not *quite* true. Let us hope, rather, that by the best cultivation of the physical world, beneath and around us; and the intellectual and moral world within us, we shall secure an individual, social, and political prosperity and happiness, whose course shall be onward and upward, and which, while the earth endures, shall not pass away.

From an address before the Wisconsin State Agricultural Society,
at Milwaukee, September 30, 1859

Rare contemporary salt print,
probably from the lost original negative made by Samuel M. Fassett, in Chicago,
October 4, 1859. National Portrait Gallery.

15

Jefferson's Principles of Free Government

Messrs. Henry L. Pierce, & others.   Springfield, Ills.
Gentlemen   April 6, 1859

. . . Soberly, it is now no child's play to save the principles of Jefferson from total overthrow in this nation.

One would start with great confidence that he could convince any sane child that the simpler propositions of Euclid are true; but, nevertheless, he would fail, utterly, with one who should deny the definitions and axioms. The principles of Jefferson are the definitions and axioms of free society. And yet they are denied, and evaded, with no small show of success. One dashingly calls them "glittering generalities"; another bluntly calls them "self evident lies"; and still others insidiously argue that they apply only to "superior races."

These expressions, differing in form, are identical in object and effect—the supplanting the principles of free government, and restoring those of classification, caste, and legitimacy. They would delight a convocation of crowned heads, plotting against the people. They are the van-guard—the miners, and sappers—of returning despotism. We must repulse them, or they will subjugate us.

This is a world of compensations; and he who would *be* no slave, must consent to *have* no slave. Those who deny freedom to others, deserve it not for themselves; and, under a just God, can not long retain it.

All honor to Jefferson—to the man who, in the concrete pressure of a struggle for national independence by a single people, had the coolness, forecast, and capacity to introduce into a merely revolutionary document, an abstract truth, applicable to all men and all times, and so to embalm it there, that to-day, and in all coming days, it shall be a rebuke and a stumbling-block to the very harbingers of re-appearing tyranny and oppression. Your obedient Servant

A. LINCOLN

*Rare contemporary salt print from the lost original negative
made by an unknown photographer, probably in Illinois, about 1859.*
Ostendorf Collection.

16

"That Right Makes Might"

If slavery is right, all words, acts, laws, and constitutions against it, are themselves wrong, and should be silenced, and swept away. If it is right, we cannot justly object to its nationality—its universality; if it is wrong, they cannot justly insist upon its extension—its enlargement. All they ask, we could readily grant, if we thought slavery right; all we ask, they could as readily grant, if they thought it wrong. Their thinking it right, and our thinking it wrong, is the precise fact upon which depends the whole controversy. Thinking it right, as they do, they are not to blame for desiring its full recognition, as being right; but, thinking it wrong, as we do, can we yield to them? Can we cast our votes with their view, and against our own? In view of our moral, social, and political responsibilities, can we do this?

Wrong as we think slavery is, we can yet afford to let it alone where it is, because that much is due to the necessity arising from its actual presence in the nation; but can we, while our votes will prevent it, allow it to spread into the National Territories, and to overrun us here in these Free States? If our sense of duty forbids this, then let us stand by our duty, fearlessly and effectively. Let us be diverted by none of those sophistical contrivances where-with we are so industriously plied and belabored—contrivances such as groping for some middle ground between the right and the wrong, vain as the search for a man who should be neither a living man nor a dead man—such as a policy of "don't care" on a question about which all true men do care—such as Union appeals beseeching true Union men to yield to Disunionists, reversing the divine rule, and calling, not the sinners, but the righteous to repentance —such as invocations to Washington, imploring men to unsay what Washington said, and undo what Washington did.

Neither let us be slandered from our duty by false accusations against us, nor frightened from it by menaces of destruction to the Government nor of dungeons to ourselves. LET US HAVE FAITH THAT RIGHT MAKES MIGHT, AND IN THAT FAITH, LET US, TO THE END, DARE TO DO OUR DUTY AS WE UNDER-STAND IT.

Conclusion of the "Cooper Institute Speech,"
at New York City, February 27, 1860

The tones, the gestures, the kindling eye, and the mirth-provoking look defy the reporter's skill. The vast assemblage frequently rang with cheers and shouts of applause. No man ever before made such an impression on his first appeal to a New York audience.

Noah Brooks, reporting for the *Chicago Tribune*
on Lincoln's "Cooper Institute Speech"

. . . my friend Brady, the photographer, insisted that his photograph of Mr. Lincoln, taken the morning of the day he made his Cooper Institute speech in New York,—much the best portrait, by the way, in circulation of him during the campaign,—was the means of his election. That it helped largely to this end I do not doubt. The effect of such influences, though silent, is powerful.

The portrait painter Francis Carpenter,
Six Months at The White House with Abraham Lincoln

Dressed for his Cooper Institute appearance, the fifty-one-year-old
Lincoln posed for the first time for Mathew Brady, in New York City,
February 27, 1860. Carte-de-visite printed by Brady's gallery
from a lost copy negative of a retouched original print.
Courtesy of Lincoln Kirstein.

Hon. L. Trumbull: Springfield,
My dear Sir   April 29. 1860

Yours of the 24th. was duly received; and I have postponed answering it, hoping by the result at Charleston, to know who is to lead our adversaries, before writing. But Charleston hangs fire, and I wait no longer.

As you request, I will be entirely frank. The taste *is* in my mouth a little; and this, no doubt, disqualifies me, to some extent, to form correct opinions. You may confidently rely, however, that by no advice or consent of mine, shall my pretensions be pressed to the point of endangering our common cause.

Now, as to my opinions about the chances of others in Illinois. I think neither Seward nor Bates can carry Illinois if Douglas shall be on the track; and that either of them can, if he shall not be. I rather think McLean could carry it with D. on or off—in other words, I think McLean is stronger in Illinois, taking all sections of it, than either S. or B; and I think S. the weakest of the three. I hear no objection to McLean, except his age; but that objection seems to occur to every one; and it is possible it might leave him no stronger than the others. By the way, if we should nominate him, how would we save to ourselves the chance of filling his vacancy in the Court? Have him

hold on up to the moment of his inauguration? Would that course be no draw-back upon us in the canvass?

Recurring to Illinois, we want something here quite as much as, and which is harder to get than, the electoral vote—the Legislature. And it is exactly in this point that Seward's nomination would be hard upon us. Suppose he should gain us a thousand votes in Winnebago, it would not compensate for the loss of fifty in Edgar.

A word now for your own special benefit. You better write no letters which can possibly be distorted into opposition, or quasi opposition to me. There are men on the constant watch for such things out of which to prejudice my peculiar friends against you. While I have no more suspicion of you than I have of my best friend living, I am kept in a constant struggle against suggestions of this sort. I have hesitated some to write this paragraph, lest you should suspect I do it for my own benefit, and not for yours; but on reflection I conclude you will not suspect me.

Let no eye but your own see this—not that there is anything wrong, or even ungenerous, in it; but it would be misconstrued. Your friend as ever

A. LINCOLN

Letter to Lincoln's friend and political ally
Senator Lyman Trumbull of Illinois

*Contemporary albumen print believed to be
the only surviving likeness printed from the lost original negative
made by William Seavy, in Springfield, Illinois, probably during the spring
or summer of 1860. Ostendorf Collection.*

18

His Law Partner Remembers Him:
Two Sketches

. . . In 1843–4 Mr. Lincoln and I became partners in the law business in Springfield, but did business in all the surrounding counties. Our partnership was never legally dissolved till the night of his assassination. The good man, the noble man, would take none of my fees made in the law business after his election to the Presidency. Mr. Lincoln was a safe councilor, a good lawyer and an honest man in all the walks of life.

. . . Mr. Lincoln was a cool, cautious, conservative, and long-headed man. Mr. Lincoln could be trusted by the people. They did trust him and they were never deceived. He was a pure man, a great man, and a patriot. In the practice of law he was simple honest, fair and broad minded. He was courteous to the bar, and to the court. He was open candid and square in his profession, never practicing on the sharp or low. Mr. Lincoln met all questions fairly, squarely, . . . making no concealments of his . . . intentions in any case. He took no snap judgments, nor used any tricks in his business. . . .

Statement by William Herndon, April 14, 1886;
cited by Alfred North in a letter to Truman Bartlett, July 1, 1887

. . . Mr. Lincoln's perceptions were slow, cold, precise and exact. Everything came to Lincoln . . . clean and clear cut, stript of all extraneous matter whatsoever. Everything came to him in its precise shape—gravity and color. . . . No lurking illusion—delusion—error, false in itself and clad for the moment in robes of splendor, woven by the imagination, ever passed unchallenged or undetected over the threshold of his mind, that divides vision from the realm and home of thought. Names to him were nothing and titles naught—assumptions always standing back abashed at his cold intellectual glare. . . . There was no . . . refraction there, in this man's brain: he was not impulsive fanciful or imaginative, but cold, calm, precise and exact: he threw his whole mental light around the object seen. . . . In his mental view he crushed the unreal, . . . the hollow and the sham: . . . he saw what no man could well dispute, but he failed to see what might be seen . . . by other men. . . . His own mind was his own and exclusive standard. . . .

William Herndon, manuscript fragment,
"Lincoln Individuality," undated

Lincoln, several days after being nominated
for the presidency of the United States. Original ambrotype
presented by Lincoln to Joseph H. Barrett and subsequently reproduced lithographically
as the frontispiece in Barrett's Life of Abraham Lincoln.
Made in Springfield, Illinois, May 20 or 24, 1860,
probably by Preston Butler. Nebraska State Historical Society.

19

Lincoln on a Speaking Tour of New England in 1860,
Prior to His Run for the Presidency

In repose, I must confess, "Long Abe's" appearance is *not* comely. But stir him up and the fire of genius plays on every feature. Listening to him, calmly and unprejudiced, I was convinced that he has no superior as a stump speaker.

A reporter for the New York *Evening Post*, 1860

Look at the magnitude of this subject! One sixth of our population, in round numbers—not quite one sixth, and yet more than a seventh, —about one sixth of the whole population of the United States are slaves! The owners of these slaves consider them property. The effect upon the minds of the owners is that of property, and nothing else—it induces them to insist upon all that will favorably affect its value as property, to demand laws and institutions and a public policy that shall increase and secure its value, and make it durable, lasting and universal. The effect on the minds of the owners is to persuade them that there is no wrong in it. The slaveholder does not like to be considered a mean fellow, for holding that species of property, and hence he has to struggle within himself and sets about arguing himself into the belief that Slavery is right. The property influences his mind. The dissenting minister, who argued some theological point with one of the established church, was always met by the reply, "I can't see it so." He opened the Bible, and pointed him to a passage, but the orthodox minister replied, "I can't see it so." Then he showed him a single word—"Can you see that?" "Yes, I see it," was the reply. The dissenter laid a guinea over the word and asked, "Do you see it now?" [Great laughter.] So here. Whether the owners of this species of property do really see it as it is, it is not for me to say, but if they do, they see it as it is through 2,000,000,000 of dollars, and that is a pretty thick coating. [Laughter.] Certain it is, that they do not see it as we see it. Certain it is, that this two thousand million of dollars, invested in this species of property, all so concentrated that the mind can grasp it at once—this immense pecuniary interest, has its influence upon their minds.

But here in Connecticut and at the North Slavery does not exist, and we see it through no such medium. To us it appears natural to think that slaves are human beings; *men*, not property; that some of

(*Continued on page 60*)

Positive printed on glass from a lost original negative or
ambrotype made by Edward A. Barnwell, in Decatur, Illinois,
May 9, 1860. (This is a cropped enlargement of
the image appearing opposite the title page.)
Decatur Public Library.

Overleaf, left: *Contemporary albumen print*
believed to be the only surviving likeness printed
from the lost original negative made by an unknown photographer,
probably in Springfield or Chicago, during the spring or summer of 1860.
Courtesy of Josephine Ross.
Right: *Solio print of a lost contemporary albumen print from the lost*
original negative made by an unknown photographer,
probably between February and August 1860.
Allegheny College.

the things, at least, stated about men in the Declaration of Independence apply to them as well as to us. [Applause.] I say, we think, most of us, that this Charter of Freedom applies to the slave as well as to ourselves, that the class of arguments put forward to batter down that idea, are also calculated to break down the very idea of a free government, even for white men, and to undermine the very foundations of free society. [Continued applause.] We think Slavery a great moral wrong, and while we do not claim the right to touch it where it exists, we wish to treat it as a wrong in the Territories, where our votes will reach it. We think that a respect for ourselves, a regard for future generations and for the God that made us, require that we put down this wrong where our votes will properly reach it. We think that species of labor an injury to free white men—in short, we think Slavery a great moral, social and political evil, tolerable only because, and so far as its actual existence makes it necessary to tolerate it, and that beyond that, it ought to be treated as a wrong.... I don't mean that we ought to attack it where it exists. To me it seems that if we were to form a government anew, in view of the actual presence of Slavery we should find it necessary to frame just such a government as our fathers did; giving to the slaveholder the entire control where the system was established, while we possessed the power to restrain it from going outside those limits. [Applause.] From the necessities of the case we should be compelled to form just such a government as our blessed fathers gave us; and, surely, if they have so made it, that adds another reason why we should let Slavery alone where it exists. . . .

Now I have spoken of a policy based on the idea that Slavery is wrong, and a policy based upon the idea that it is right. But an effort has been made for a policy that shall treat it as neither right or wrong. It is based upon utter indifference. Its leading advocate has said "I don't care whether it be voted up or down." [Laughter.] "It is merely a matter of dollars and cents." "The Almighty has drawn a line across this continent, on one side of which all soil must forever be cultivated by slave labor, and on the other by free;" "when the struggle is between the white man and the negro, I am for the white man; when it is between the negro and the crocodile, I am for the negro." Its central idea is indifference. It holds that it makes no more difference to us whether the Territories become free or slave States, than whether my neighbor stocks his farm with horned cattle or puts it into tobacco. All recognize this policy, the plausible sugar-coated name of which is *popular sovereignty.* [Laughter.]

This policy chiefly stands in the way of a permanent settlement of the question. I believe there is no danger of its becoming the permanent policy of the country, for it is based on a public indifference. There is nobody that "don't care." ALL THE PEOPLE DO CARE! one way or the other. [Great applause.] I do not charge that its author, when he says he "don't care," states his individual opinion; he only expresses his policy for the government. I understand that he has never said, as an individual, whether he thought Slavery right or wrong—and he is the only man in the nation that has not! Now such a policy may have a temporary run; it may spring up as necessary to the political prospects of some gentleman; but it is utterly baseless; the people are not indifferent; and it can therefore have no durability or permanence. . . .

From a speech at New Haven, Connecticut, March 6, 1860

20

The Nigger and the Crocodile;
The Rattlesnake of Slavery

The proposition that there is a struggle between the white man and the negro contains a falsehood. There is *no* struggle between them. It assumes that unless the white man enslaves the negro, the negro will enslave the white man. In that case, I think I would go for enslaving the black man, in preference to being enslaved myself. As the learned Judge of a certain Court is said to have decided—"When a ship is wrecked at sea, and two men seize upon one plank which is capable of sustaining but one of them, either of them can rightfully push the other off!" There is, however, no such controversy here. They say that between the nigger and the crocodile they go for the nigger. The proportion, therefore, is, that as the crocodile to the nigger so is the nigger to the white man. . . .

If, then, we of the Republican party who think slavery is a wrong, and would mould public opinion to the fact that it is wrong, should get the control of the general government, I do not say we would or should meddle with it where it exists; but we could inaugurate a policy which would treat it as a wrong, and prevent its extension.

For instance, out in the street, or in the field, or on the prairie I find a rattlesnake. I take a stake and kill him. Everybody would applaud the act and say I did right. But suppose the snake was in a bed where children were sleeping. Would I do right to strike him there? I might hurt the children; or I might not kill, but only arouse and exasperate the snake, and he might bite the children. Thus, by meddling with him here, I would do more hurt than good. Slavery is like this. We dare not strike at it where it is. The manner in which our constitution is framed constrains us from making war upon it where it already exists. The question that we now have to deal with is, "Shall we be acting right to take this snake and carry it to a bed where there are children?" The Republican party insists upon keeping it out of the bed.

From a speech at Hartford, Connecticut, March 5, 1860

Rare contemporary albumen print
from the lost original negative made by an unknown photographer,
probably in Springfield, Illinois, during the spring or summer of 1860.
Lincoln National Life Foundation.

It was just after his controversy with Douglas, and some months before the meeting of the Chicago Convention of 1860, that Mr. Lincoln came to Norwich [Connecticut] to make a political speech....

The next morning I met him at the railroad station, where he was conversing with our Mayor, every few minutes looking up the track and inquiring, half impatiently and half quizzically, "Where's that 'wagon' of yours? Why don't the 'wagon' come along?" On being introduced to him, he fixed his eyes upon me, and said: "I have seen you before, sir!" "I think not," I replied; "you must mistake me for some other person." "No, I don't; I saw you at the Town Hall, last evening." "Is it possible, Mr. Lincoln, that you could observe individuals so closely in such a crowd?" "Oh, yes!" he replied, laughing; "that is my way. I don't forget faces. Were you not there?" "I was, sir, and I was well paid for going"; adding, somewhat in the vein of pleasantry he had started, "I consider it one of the most extraordinary speeches I ever heard."

As we entered the cars, he beckoned me to take a seat with him, and said, in a most agreeably frank way, "Were you sincere in what you said about my speech just now?" "I meant every word of it, Mr. Lincoln. Why, an old dyed-in-the-wool Democrat, who sat near me, applauded you repeatedly; and, when rallied upon his conversion to sound principles, answered, 'I don't believe a word he says, but I can't help clapping him, he is so *pat!*' That I call the triumph of oratory,—

> When you convince a man against his will,
> Though he is of the same opinion still.

Indeed, sir, I learned more of the art of public speaking last evening than I could from a whole course of lectures on Rhetoric."

"Ah! that reminds me," said he, "of a most extraordinary circumstance which occurred in New Haven the other day. They told me that the Professor of Rhetoric in Yale College,—a very learned man, isn't he?"

"Yes, sir, and a fine critic too."

"Well, I suppose so; he ought to be, at any rate,—they told me that he came to hear me, and took notes of my speech, and gave a lecture on it to his class the next day; and, not satisfied with that, he followed me up to Meriden the next evening, and heard me again for the same purpose. Now, if this is so, it is to my mind very extraordinary. I have been sufficiently astonished at my success in the West. It has been most unexpected. But I had no thought of any marked success at the East, and least of all that I should draw out such com-

mendations from literary and learned men. Now," he continued, "I should like very much to know what it was in my speech you thought so remarkable, and what you suppose interested my friend, the Professor, so much."

"The clearness of your statements, Mr. Lincoln; the unanswerable style of your reasoning, and especially your illustrations, which were romance and pathos, and fun and logic all welded together. That story about the snakes, for example, which set the hands and feet of your Democratic hearers in such vigorous motion, was at once queer and comical, and tragic and argumentative. It broke through all the barriers of a man's previous opinions and prejudices at a crash, and blew up the very citadel of his false theories before he could know what had hurt him."

"Can you remember any other illustrations," said he, "of this peculiarity of my style?"

I gave him others of the same sort, occupying some half-hour in the critique, when he said: "I am much obliged to you for this. I have been wishing for a long time to find some one who would make this analysis for me. It throws light on a subject which has been dark to me. I can understand very readily how such a power as you have ascribed to me will account for the effect which seems to be produced by my speeches. I hope you have not been too flattering in your estimate. Certainly, I have had a most wonderful success, for a man of my limited education."

"That suggests, Mr. Lincoln, an inquiry which has several times been upon my lips during this conversation. I want very much to know how you got this unusual power of 'putting things.' It must have been a matter of education. No man has it by nature alone. What has your education been?"

"Well, as to education, the newspapers are correct; I never went to school more than six months in my life. But, as you say, this must be a product of culture in some form. I have been putting the question you ask me to myself, while you have been talking. I can say this, that among my earliest recollections I remember how, when a mere child, I used to get irritated when any body talked to me in a way I could not understand. I don't think I ever got angry at anything else in my life. But that always disturbed my temper, and has ever since. I can remember going to my little bedroom, after hearing the neighbors talk of an evening with my father, and spending no small part of the night walking up and down, and trying to make out what was the exact meaning of some of their, to me, dark sayings. I could not

(*Continued on page 67*)

sleep, though I often tried to, when I got on such a hunt after an idea, until I had caught it; and when I thought I had got it, I was not satisfied until I had repeated it over and over, until I had put it in language plain enough, as I thought, for any boy I knew to comprehend. This was a kind of passion with me, and it has stuck by me; for I am never easy now, when I am handling a thought, till I have bounded it North, and bounded it South, and bounded it East, and bounded it West. Perhaps that accounts for the characteristic you observe in my speeches, though I never put the two things together before."

"Mr. Lincoln, I thank you for this. It is the most splendid educational fact I ever happened upon. This is *genius*, with all its impulsive, inspiring, dominating power over the mind of its possessor, developed by education into *talent*, with its uniformity, its permanence, and its disciplined strength,—always ready, always available, never capricious,—the highest possession of the human intellect. But, let me ask, did you prepare for your profession?"

"Oh, yes! I 'read law,' as the phrase is; that is, I became a lawyer's clerk in Springfield, and copied tedious documents, and picked up what I could of law in the intervals of other work. But your question reminds me of a bit of education I had, which I am bound in honesty to mention. In the course of my law-reading, I constantly came upon the word *demonstrate*. I thought at first that I understood its meaning, but soon became satisfied that I did not. I said to myself, 'What do I mean when I *demonstrate* more than when I *reason* or *prove*? How does *demonstration* differ from any other proof?' I consulted Webster's Dictionary. That told of 'certain proof,' 'proof beyond the possibility of doubt'; but I could form no idea what sort of proof that was. I thought a great many things were proved beyond a possibility of doubt, without recourse to any such extraordinary process of reasoning as I understood 'demonstration' to be. I consulted all the dictionaries and books of reference I could find, but with no better results. You might as well have defined *blue* to a blind man. At last I said, 'Lincoln, you can never make a lawyer if you do not understand what *demonstrate* means'; and I left my situation in Springfield, went home to my father's house, and stayed there till I could give any proposition in the six books of Euclid at sight. I then found out what 'demonstrate' means, and went back to my law-studies."

I could not refrain from saying, in my admiration at such a development of character and genius combined: "Mr. Lincoln, your success is no longer a marvel. It is the legitimate result of adequate causes. You deserve it all, and a great deal more. If you will permit me, I would like to use this fact publicly. It will be most valuable in inciting our young men to that patient classical and mathematical culture which most minds absolutely require. No man can talk well unless he is able first of all to define to himself what he is talking about. Euclid, well studied, would free the world of half its calamities, by banishing half the nonsense which now deludes and curses it. I have often thought that Euclid would be one of the best books to put on the catalogue of the Tract Society, if they could only get people to read it. It would be a means of grace."

"I think so," said he, laughing; "I vote for Euclid."

Just then a gentleman entered the car who was well known as a very ardent friend of Douglas. Being a little curious to see how Mr. Lincoln would meet him, I introduced him after this fashion:—"Mr. Lincoln, allow me to introduce Mr. L——, a very particular friend of your particular friend, Mr. Douglas." He at once took his hand in a most cordial manner, saying: "I have no doubt you think you are right, sir." This hearty tribute to the honesty of a political opponent, with the manner of doing it, struck me as a beautiful exhibition of a large-hearted charity, of which we see far too little in this debating, fermenting world.

As we neared the end of our journey, Mr. Lincoln turned to me very pleasantly, and said: "I want to thank you for this conversation. I have enjoyed it very much." I replied, referring to some stalwart denunciations he had just been uttering of the demoralizing influences of Washington upon Northern politicians in respect to the slavery question, "Mr. Lincoln, may I say one thing to you before we separate?"

"Certainly, anything you please."

"You have just spoken of the tendency of political life in Washington to debase the moral convictions of our representatives there by the admixture of considerations of mere political expediency. You have become, by the controversy with Mr. Douglas, one of our leaders in this great struggle with slavery, which is undoubtedly *the* struggle of the nation and the age. What I would like to say is this, and I say it with a full heart, *Be true to your principles and we will be true to you, and God will be true to us all!*" His homely face lighted up instantly with a beaming expression, and taking my hand warmly in both of his, he said: "I say *Amen* to that—AMEN to that!"

The Reverend J. P. Gulliver,
in an article for the New York *Independent*,
September 1, 1864

Contemporary albumen print from a lost contemporary negative
of a pose believed to have been made by William Shaw, probably
in Chicago or Springfield, during the spring or summer of 1860.
Mellon Collection.

22

Sketch for a Campaign Biography
(*Written by Lincoln in the Third Person*)

Abraham Lincoln was born Feb. 12, 1809, then in Hardin, now in the more recently formed county of Larue, Kentucky. His father, Thomas, & grand-father, Abraham, were born in Rockingham county Virginia, whither their ancestors had come from Berks county Pennsylvania. His lineage has been traced no farther back than this. The family were originally quakers, though in later times they have fallen away from the peculiar habits of that people. . . .

The present subject has no brother or sister of the whole or half blood. He had a sister, older than himself, who was grown and married, but died many years ago, leaving no child. Also a brother, younger than himself, who died in infancy. Before leaving Kentucky he and his sister were sent for short periods, to A.B.C. schools, the first kept by Zachariah Riney, and the second by Caleb Hazel.

At this time his father resided on Knob-creek, on the road from Bardstown Ky. to Nashville Tenn. at a point three, or three and a half miles South or South-West of Atherton's ferry on the Rolling Fork. From this place he removed to what is now Spencer county Indiana, in the autumn of 1816, A. then being in his eighth year. This removal was partly on account of slavery; but chiefly on account of the difficulty in land titles in Ky. He settled in an unbroken forest; and the clearing away of surplus wood was the great task ahead. A. though very young, was large of his age, and had an axe put into his hands at once; and from that till within his twentythird year, he was almost constantly handling that most useful instrument—less, of course, in plowing and harvesting seasons. At this place A. took an early start as a hunter, which was never much improved afterwards. (A few days before the completion of his eighth year, in the absence of his father, a flock of wild turkeys approached the new log-cabin, and A. with a rifle gun, standing inside, shot through a crack, and killed one of them. He has never since pulled a trigger on any larger game.) In the autumn of 1818 his mother died; and a year afterwards his father married Mrs. Sally Johnston, at Elizabeth-Town, Ky—a widow, with three children of her first marriage. She proved a good and kind mother to A. and is still living in Coles Co. Illinois. There were no children of this second marriage. His father's residence continued at the same place in Indiana, till 1830. While here A. went to A.B.C. schools by littles, kept successively by Andrew Crawford, —— Sweeney, and Azel W. Dorsey. He does not remember any other. The family of Mr. Dorsey now reside in Schuyler Co. Illinois. A. now thinks that the aggregate of all his schooling did not amount to one year. He was never in a college or academy as a student, and never inside of a college or academy building till since he had a law-license. What he has in the way of education, he has picked up. After he was twentythree, and had separated from his father, he studied English grammar, imperfectly of course, but so as to speak and write as well as he now does. He studied and nearly mastered the Six-books of Euclid, since he was a member of Congress. He regrets his want of education, and does what he can to supply the want. In his tenth year he was kicked by a horse, and apparently killed for a time. When he was nineteen, still residing in Indiana, he made his first trip upon a flat-boat to New-Orleans. He was a hired hand merely; and he and a son of the owner, without other assistance, made the trip. The nature of part of the cargo-load, as it was called—made it necessary for them to linger and trade along the Sugar coast—and one night they were attacked by seven negroes with intent to kill and rob them. They were hurt some in the melee, but succeeded in driving the negroes from the boat, and then "cut cable" "weighed anchor" and left.

March 1st. 1830—A. having just completed his 21st. year, his father and family, with the families of the two daughters and sons-in-law, of his step-mother, left the old homestead in Indiana, and came to Illinois. Their mode of conveyance was waggons drawn by ox-teams, or A. drove one of the teams. They reached the county of Macon, and stopped there some time within the same month of March. His father and family settled a new place on the North side of the Sangamon river, at the junction of the timber-land and prairie, about ten miles westerly from Decatur. Here they built a log-cabin, into which they removed, and made sufficient of rails to fence ten acres of ground, fenced and broke the ground, and raised a crop of sown corn upon it the same year. These are, or are supposed to be, the rails about which so much is being said just now, though they are far from being the first, or only rails ever made by A.

(*Continued on page 70*)

Rare contemporary albumen print
from the lost original negative made by Alexander Hesler, in Springfield,
Illinois, June 3, 1860. Ostendorf Collection.

The sons-in-law were temporarily settled at other places in the county. In the autumn all hands were greatly afflicted with ague and fever, to which they had not been used, and by which they were greatly discouraged—so much so that they determined on leaving the county. They remained however, through the succeeding winter, which was the winter of the very celebrated "deep snow" of Illinois. During that winter, A. together with his step-mother's son, John D. Johnston, and John Hanks, yet residing in Macon county, hired themselves to one Denton Offutt, to take a flat boat from Beardstown Illinois to New-Orleans, and for that purpose, were to join him—Offutt—at Springfield, Ills. so soon as the snow should go off. When it did go off which was about the 1st. of March 1831—the county was so flooded, as to make traveling by land impracticable; to obviate which difficulty they purchased a large canoe and came down the Sangamon river in it. This is the time and the manner of A's first entrance into Sangamon County. They found Offutt at Springfield, but learned from him that he had failed in getting a boat at Beardstown. This led to their hiring themselves to him at $12 per month, each, and getting the timber out of the trees and building a boat at old Sangamon Town on the Sangamon river, seven miles N.W. of Springfield, which boat they took to New-Orleans, substantially upon the old contract. It was in connection with this boat that occurred the ludicrous incident of sewing up the hogs' eyes. Offutt bought thirty odd large fat live hogs, but found difficulty in driving them from where [he] purchased them to the boat, and thereupon conceived the whim that he could sew up their eyes and drive them where he pleased. No sooner thought of than decided, he put his hands, including A. at the job, which they completed—all but the driving. In their blind condition they could not be driven out of the lot or field they were in. This expedient failing, they were tied and hauled on carts to the boat. It was near the Sangamon River, within what is now Menard county.

During this boat enterprise acquaintance with Offutt, who was previously an entire stranger, he conceived a liking for A. and believing he could turn him to account, he contracted with him to act as clerk for him, on his return from New-Orleans, in charge of a store

and Mill at New-Salem, then in Sangamon, now in Menard county. Hanks had not gone to New-Orleans, but having a family, and being likely to be detained from home longer than at first expected, had turned back from St. Louis. He is the same John Hanks who now engineers the "rail enterprise" at Decatur; and is a first cousin to A's mother. A's father, with his own family & others mentioned, had, in pursuance of their intention, removed from Macon to Coles county. John D. Johnston, the step-mother's son, went to them; and A. stopped indefinitely, and, for the first time, as it were, by himself at New-Salem, before mentioned. This was in July 1831. Here he rapidly made acquaintances and friends. In less than a year Offutt's business was failing—had almost failed,—when the Black-Hawk war of 1832—broke out. A. joined a volunteer company, and to his own surprise, was elected captain of it. He says he has not since had any success in life which gave him so much satisfaction. He went the campaign, served near three months, met the ordinary hardships of such an expedition, but was in no battle. He now owns in Iowa the land upon which his own warrants for this service were located. Returning from the campaign, and encouraged by his great popularity among his immediate neighbors, he, the same year, ran for the Legislature and was beaten—his own precinct, however, casting its votes 277 for and 7 against him. And this too while he was an avowed Clay man, and the precinct the autumn afterwards, giving a majority of 115 to Genl. Jackson over Mr. Clay. This was the only time A. was ever beaten on a direct vote of the people. He was now without means and out of business, but was anxious to remain with his friends who had treated him with so much generosity especially as he had nothing elsewhere to go to. He studied what he should do —thought of learning the black-smith trade—thought of trying to study law—rather thought he could not succeed at that without a better education. Before long, strangely enough, a man offered to sell, and did sell, to A., and another as poor as himself, an old stock of goods, upon credit. They opened as merchants; and he says that was *the* store. Of course they did nothing but get deeper and deeper in debt. He was appointed Postmaster at New-Salem—the office being too insignificant, to make his politics an objection. The store winked

(*Continued on page 72*)

Gelatin silver print of a lost faded contemporary albumen print
from the lost original negative made by Joseph Hill,
in Springfield, Illinois, during late May or early June 1860.
Mellon Collection.

out. The Surveyor of Sangamon, offered to depute to A. that portion of his work which was within his part of the county. He accepted, procured a compass and chain, studied Flint, and Gibson a little, and went at it. This procured bread, and kept soul and body together. The election of 1834 came, and he was then elected to the Legislature by the highest vote cast for any candidate. Major John T. Stuart, then in full practice of the law, was also elected. During the canvass, in a private conversation he encouraged A. to study law. After the election he borrowed books of Stuart, took them home with him, and went at it in good earnest. He studied with nobody. He still mixed in the surveying to pay board and clothing bills. When the Legislature met, the law books were dropped, but were taken up again at the end of the session. He was re-elected in 1836, 1838, and 1840. In the autumn of 1836 he obtained a law licence, and on April 15, 1837 removed to Springfield, and commenced the practice, his old friend, Stuart, taking him into partnership. March 3rd. 1837, by a protest entered upon the Ills. House Journal of that date, at pages 817, 818, A. with Dan Stone, another representative of Sangamon, briefly defined his position on the slavery question; and so far as it goes, it was then the same that it is now. The protest is as follows—(Here insert it). In 1838, & 1840 Mr. L's party in the Legislature voted for him as Speaker; but being in the minority, he was not elected. After 1840 he declined a re-election to the Legislature. He was on the Harrison electoral ticket in 1840, and on that of Clay in 1844, and spent much time and labor in both those canvasses. In Nov. 1842 he was married to Mary, daughter of Robert S. Todd, of Lexington, Kentucky. They have three living children, all sons—one born in 1843, one in 1850, and one in 1853. They lost one, who was born in 1846. In 1846, he was elected to the lower House of Congress, and served one term only, commencing in Dec. 1847 and ending with the inauguration of Gen. Taylor, in March 1849. All the battles of the Mexican war had been fought before Mr. L. took his seat in congress, but the American army was still in Mexico, and the treaty of peace was not fully and formally ratified till the June afterwards. Much has been said of his course in Congress in regard to this war. A careful examination of the Journals and Congressional Globe shows that he voted for all the supply measures which came up, and for all the measures in any way favorable to the officers, soldiers, and their families, who conducted the war through; with this exception that some of these measures passed without yeas and nays, leaving no record as to how particular men voted. The Journals and Globe also show him voting that the war was unnecessarily and unconstitutionally begun by the President of the United States. . . .

In 1848, during his term in congress, he advocated Gen. Taylor's nomination for the Presidency, in opposition to all others, and also took an active part for his election, after his nomination—speaking a few times in Maryland, near Washington, several times in Massachusetts, and canvassing quite fully his own district in Illinois, which was followed by a majority in the district of over 1500 for Gen. Taylor.

Upon his return from Congress he went to the practice of the law with greater earnestness than ever before. In 1852 he was upon the Scott electoral ticket, and did something in the way of canvassing, but owing to the hopelessness of the cause in Illinois, he did less than in previous presidential canvasses.

In 1854, his profession had almost superseded the thought of politics in his mind, when the repeal of the Missouri compromise aroused him as he had never been before.

In the autumn of that year he took the stump with no broader practical aim or object than to secure, if possible, the reelection of Hon Richard Yates to congress. His speeches at once attracted a more marked attention than they had ever before done. As the canvass proceeded, he was drawn to different parts of the state, outside of Mr. Yates' district. He did not abandon the law, but gave his attention, by turns, to that and politics. The State agricultural fair was at Springfield that year, and Douglas was announced to speak there.

In the canvass of 1856, Mr. L. made over fifty speeches, no one of which, so far as he remembers, was put in print. One of them was made at Galena, but Mr. L. has no recollection of any part of it being printed; nor does he remember whether in that speech he said anything about a Supreme court decision. He may have spoken upon that subject; and some of the newspapers may have reported him as saying what is now ascribed to him; but he thinks he could not have expressed himself as represented.

Autograph document, unsigned;
written about June 1860 for use by John Scripps
in preparing a campaign biography

The fifty-one-year-old presidential candidate.
Believed to be the only surviving original of the half
dozen ambrotypes made by Preston Butler, in Springfield, Illinois,
August 13, 1860, for use by the miniature portraitist
John Henry Brown. Library of Congress.

Lincoln's Farewell Address at
Springfield, February 11, 1861

My friends—No one, not in my situation, can appreciate my feeling of
sadness at this parting. To this place, and the kindness of these people, I
owe every thing. Here I have lived a quarter of a century, and have passed
from a young to an old man. Here my children have been born, and one is
buried. I now leave, not knowing when, or whether ever, I may return,
with a task before me greater than that which rested upon Washington.
Without the assistance of that Divine Being, who ever attended him, I
cannot succeed. With that assistance I cannot fail. Trusting in Him, who
can go with me, and remain with you and be every where for good, let us
confidently hope that all will yet be well. To His care commending you,
as I hope in your prayers you will commend me, I bid you an affectionate
farewell.

Delivered from the back of the special train that was to take
Lincoln to Washington for his inauguration

. . . An ominous incident of mysterious character, he said, occurred
just after his election in 1860. It was the double image of himself in a
looking-glass, which he saw while lying on a lounge in his own
chamber at Springfield. There was Abraham Lincoln's face reflecting
the full glow of health and hopeful life; and in the same mirror, at the
same moment of time, was the face of Abraham Lincoln showing a
ghostly paleness. On trying the experiment at other times, as con-
firmatory tests, the illusion reappeared, and then vanished as before.

Mr. Lincoln more than once told me that he could not explain
this phenomenon; that he had tried to reproduce the double reflection
at the Executive Mansion, but without success; that it had worried
him not a little; and that the mystery had its meaning, which was
clear enough to him. To his mind the illusion was a sign,—the lifelike image betokening a safe passage through his first term as President; the ghostly one, that death would overtake him before the close
of the second.

Ward Lamon, *Recollections of Abraham Lincoln*

*Contemporary albumen print from the lost original negative
made in Springfield, Illinois, May 20, 1860,
probably by Preston Butler.* Brown University.

En Route to Washington, Lincoln Addresses the New Jersey Senate

May I be pardoned if, upon this occasion, I mention that away back in my childhood, the earliest days of my being able to read, I got hold of a small book, such a one as few of the younger members have ever seen, "Weems's Life of Washington." I remember all the accounts there given of the battle fields and struggles for the liberties of the country, and none fixed themselves upon my imagination so deeply as the struggle here at Trenton, New-Jersey. The crossing of the river; the contest with the Hessians; the great hardships endured at that time, all fixed themselves on my memory more than any single revolutionary event; and you all know, for you have all been boys, how these early impressions last longer than any others. I recollect thinking then, boy even though I was, that there must have been something more than common that those men struggled for. I am exceedingly anxious that that thing which they struggled for; that something even more than National Independence; that something that held out a great promise to all the people of the world to all time to come; I am exceedingly anxious that this Union, the Constitution, and the liberties of the people shall be perpetuated in accordance with the original idea for which that struggle was made, and I shall be most happy indeed if I shall be an humble instrument in the hands of the Almighty, and of this, his almost chosen people, for perpetuating the object of that great struggle.

From a speech at Trenton, New Jersey, February 21, 1861

Gelatin silver print of a lost albumen print
from the lost original negative made by Alexander Hesler, in Springfield,
Illinois, June 3, 1860. Mellon Collection.

Overleaf, left and right: *"There is the peculiar curve of the lower lip,*
the lone mole on the right cheek, and a pose of the head
so essentially Lincolnian; no other artist has ever caught it,"
wrote Lincoln's law partner, William Herndon,
of the profile pose (left). *Reproduced from gelatin silver prints*
of two positives printed on glass, about 1900,
from the original negatives (see pages 10 and 11) *made by Alexander Hesler,*
in Springfield, Illinois, June 3, 1860. Mellon Collection.

PHOTOGRAPHED BY C. S. GERMAN,
NATIONAL GALLERY, WEST SIDE SQUARE, SPRINGFIELD, ILL.

25

The First Inaugural Address
March 4, 1861

Fellow citizens of the United States:

In compliance with a custom as old as the government itself, I appear before you to address you briefly, and to take, in your presence, the oath prescribed by the Constitution of the United States, to be taken by the President "before he enters on the execution of his office."

I do not consider it necessary, at present, for me to discuss those matters of administration about which there is no special anxiety, or excitement.

Apprehension seems to exist among the people of the Southern States, that by the accession of a Republican Administration, their property, and their peace, and personal security, are to be endangered. There has never been any reasonable cause for such apprehension. Indeed, the most ample evidence to the contrary has all the while existed, and been open to their inspection. It is found in nearly all the published speeches of him who now addresses you. I do but quote from one of those speeches when I declare that "I have no purpose, directly or indirectly, to interfere with the institution of slavery in the States where it exists. I believe I have no lawful right to do so, and I have no inclination to do so." Those who nominated and elected me did so with full knowledge that I had made this, and many similar declarations, and had never recanted them. And more than this, they placed in the platform, for my acceptance, and as a law to themselves, and to me, the clear and emphatic resolution which I now read:

"*Resolved*, That the maintenance inviolate of the rights of the States, and especially the right of each State to order and control its own domestic institutions according to its own judgment exclusively, is essential to that balance of power on which the perfection and endurance of our political fabric depend; and we denounce the lawless invasion by armed force of the soil of any State or Territory, no matter under what pretext, as among the gravest of crimes."

I now reiterate these sentiments: and in doing so, I only press upon the public attention the most conclusive evidence of which the case is susceptible, that the property, peace and security of no section are to be in anywise endangered by the now incoming Administration. I add too, that all the protection which, consistently with the Constitution and the laws, can be given, will be cheerfully given to all the States when lawfully demanded, for whatever cause—as cheerfully to one section, as to another. . . .

It is seventy-two years since the first inauguration of a President under our national Constitution. During that period fifteen different and greatly distinguished citizens, have, in succession, administered the executive branch of the government. They have conducted it through many perils; and, generally, with great success. Yet, with all this scope for precedent, I now enter upon the same task for the brief constitutional term of four years, under great and peculiar difficulty. A disruption of the Federal Union heretofore only menaced, is now formidably attempted.

(*Continued on page 84*)

The President-elect, two days before he left Springfield
en route to Washington, D.C., for his inauguration.
Rare contemporary albumen print from the lost original negative
made by Christopher S. German, in Springfield, Illinois, February 9, 1861.
Lincoln National Life Foundation.

Page 80: *The earliest known likeness of Lincoln with a beard;*
made three weeks after his election to the presidency of the United States.
Gelatin silver print of a carte-de-visite print of what appears to have been a retouched
contemporary albumen print supposedly from the lost original negative made
by Samuel G. Alschuler, in Chicago, November 25, 1860.
Meserve Collection.
Page 81: *Contemporary albumen print*
from the lost original negative made by Christopher S. German,
in Springfield, Illinois, January 13, 1861, for use by
the sculptor Thomas Jones. Mellon Collection.

I hold, that in contemplation of universal law, and of the Constitution, the Union of these States is perpetual. Perpetuity is implied, if not expressed, in the fundamental law of all national governments. It is safe to assert that no government proper, ever had a provision in its organic law for its own termination. Continue to execute all the express provisions of our national Constitution, and the Union will endure forever—it being impossible to destroy it, except by some action not provided for in the instrument itself.

Again, if the United States be not a government proper, but an association of States in the nature of contract merely, can it, as a contract, be peaceably unmade, by less than all the parties who made it? One party to a contract may violate it—break it, so to speak; but does it not require all to lawfully rescind it? . . .

It follows from these views that no State, upon its own mere motion, can lawfully get out of the Union,—that *resolves* and *ordinances* to that effect are legally void; and that acts of violence, within any State or States, against the authority of the United States, are insurrectionary or revolutionary, according to circumstances.

I therefore consider that, in view of the Constitution and the laws, the Union is unbroken; and, to the extent of my ability, I shall take care, as the Constitution itself expressly enjoins upon me, that the laws of the Union be faithfully executed in all the States. Doing this I deem to be only a simple duty on my part; and I shall perform it, so far as practicable, unless my rightful masters, the American people, shall withhold the requisite means, or, in some authoritative manner, direct the contrary. I trust this will not be regarded as a menace, but only as the declared purpose of the Union that it *will* constitutionally defend, and maintain itself.

In doing this there needs to be no bloodshed or violence; and there shall be none, unless it be forced upon the national authority. The power confided to me, will be used to hold, occupy, and possess the property, and places belonging to the government, and to collect the duties and imposts; but beyond what may be necessary for these objects, there will be no invasion—no using of force against, or among the people anywhere. . . .

That there are persons in one section, or another who seek to destroy the Union at all events, and are glad of any pretext to do it, I will neither affirm or deny; but if there be such, I need address no word to them. To those, however, who really love the Union, may I not speak?

Before entering upon so grave a matter as the destruction of our national fabric, with all its benefits, its memories, and its hopes, would it not be wise to ascertain precisely why we do it? Will you hazard so desperate a step, while there is any possibility that any portion of the ills you fly from, have no real existence? Will you, while the certain ills you fly to, are greater than all the real ones you fly from? Will you risk the commission of so fearful a mistake? . . .

Plainly, the central idea of secession, is the essence of anarchy. A majority, held in restraint by constitutional checks, and limitations, and always changing easily, with deliberate changes of popular opinions and sentiments, is the only true sovereign of a free people. Whoever rejects it, does, of necessity, fly to anarchy or to despotism. Unanimity is impossible; the rule of a minority, as a permanent arrangement, is wholly inadmissable; so that, rejecting the majority principle, anarchy, or despotism in some form, is all that is left. . . .

One section of our country believes slavery is *right*, and ought to be extended, while the other believes it is *wrong*, and ought not to be extended. This is the only substantial dispute. . . .

Physically speaking, we cannot separate. We cannot remove our respective sections from each other, nor build an impassable wall between them. A husband and wife may be divorced, and go out of the presence, and beyond the reach of each other; but the different parts of our country cannot do this. They cannot but remain face to face; and intercourse, either amicable or hostile, must continue between them. Is it possible then to make that intercourse more advantageous, or more satisfactory, *after* separation than *before*? Can aliens make treaties easier than friends can make laws? Can treaties be more faithfully enforced between aliens, than laws can among friends? Suppose you go to war, you cannot fight always; and when, after much loss on both sides, and no gain on either, you cease fighting, the identical old questions, as to terms of intercourse, are again upon you.

This country, with its institutions, belongs to the people who inhabit it. Whenever they shall grow weary of the existing government, they can exercise their *constitutional* right of amending it, or their *revolutionary* right to dismember, or overthrow it. I can not be ignorant of the fact that many worthy, and patriotic citizens are desirous of having the national constitution amended. While I make no recommendation of amendments, I fully recognize the rightful authority of the people over the whole subject, to be exercised in either of the modes prescribed in the instrument itself; and I should, under existing circumstances, favor, rather than oppose, a fair opportunity being afforded the people to act upon it. . . .

The Chief Magistrate derives all his authority from the people, and they have conferred none upon him to fix terms for the separation of the States. The people themselves can do this also if they choose; but the executive, as such, has nothing to do with it. His duty is to administer the present government, as it came to his hands, and to transmit it, unimpaired by him, to his successor.

Why should there not be a patient confidence in the ultimate justice of the people? Is there any better, or equal hope, in the world? In our present differences, is either party without faith of being in the

(*Continued on page 87*)

Rare contemporary albumen print from a lost negative,
possibly the original made by Christopher S. German, in Springfield, Illinois,
February 9, 1861. Ostendorf Collection.

right? If the Almighty Ruler of nations, with his eternal truth and justice, be on your side of the North, or on yours of the South, that truth, and that justice, will surely prevail, by the judgment of this great tribunal, the American people.

By the frame of the government under which we live, this same people have wisely given their public servants but little power for mischief; and have, with equal wisdom, provided for the return of that little to their own hands at very short intervals.

While the people retain their virtue, and vigilance, no administration, by any extreme of wickedness or folly, can very seriously injure the government, in the short space of four years.

My countrymen, one and all, think calmly and *well*, upon this whole subject. Nothing valuable can be lost by taking time. If there be an object to ·hurry any of you, in hot haste, to a step which you would never take *deliberately*, that object will be frustrated by taking time; but no good object can be frustrated by it. Such of you as are now dissatisfied, still have the old Constitution unimpaired, and, on the sensitive point, the laws of your own framing under it; while the new administration will have no immediate power, if it would, to change either. If it were admitted that you who are dissatisfied, hold the right side in the dispute, there still is no single good reason for precipitate action. Intelligence, patriotism, Christianity, and a firm reliance on Him, who has never yet forsaken this favored land, are still competent to adjust, in the best way, all our present difficulty.

In *your* hands, my dissatisfied fellow countrymen, and not in *mine*, is the momentous issue of civil war. The government will not assail *you*. You can have no conflict, without being yourselves the aggressors. *You* have no oath registered in Heaven to destroy the government, while *I* shall have the most solemn one to "preserve, protect and defend" it.

I am loth to close. We are not enemies, but friends. We must not be enemies. Though passion may have strained, it must not break our bonds of affection. The mystic chords of memory, stretching from every battle-field, and patriot grave, to every living heart and hearthstone, all over this broad land, will yet swell the chorus of the Union, when again touched, as surely they will be, by the better angels of our nature.

The fifty-two-year-old President-elect in Washington, D.C.,
several days before his inauguration. Reproduced from a positive
printed on film from one frame of the original multiple-image stereographic negative
made by Alexander Gardner at Mathew Brady's gallery,
about February 24, 1861. Meserve Collection.

26

It is thus seen that the assault upon, and reduction of, Fort Sumter, was, in no sense, a matter of self defence on the part of the assailants. They well knew that the garrison in the Fort could, by no possibility, commit aggression upon them. They knew—they were expressly notified—that the giving of bread to the few brave and hungry men of the garrison, was all which would on that occasion be attempted, unless themselves, by resisting so much, should provoke more. They knew that this Government desired to keep the garrison in the Fort, not to assail them, but merely to maintain visible possession, and thus to preserve the Union from actual, and immediate dissolution— trusting, as herein-before stated, to time, discussion, and the ballot-box, for final adjustment; and they assailed, and reduced the Fort, for precisely the reverse object—to drive out the visible authority of the Federal Union, and thus force it to immediate dissolution.

That this was their object, the Executive well understood; and having said to them in the inaugural address, "You can have no conflict without being yourselves the aggressors," he took pains, not only to keep this declaration good, but also to keep the case so free from the power of ingenious sophistry, as that the world should not be able to misunderstand it. By the affair at Fort Sumter, with its surrounding circumstances, that point was reached. Then, and thereby, the assailants of the Government, began the conflict of arms, without a gun in sight, or in expectancy, to return their fire, save only the few in the Fort, sent to that harbor, years before, for their own protection, and still ready to give that protection, in whatever was lawful. In this act, discarding all else, they have forced upon the country, the distinct issue: "Immediate dissolution, or blood."

And this issue embraces more than the fate of these United States. It presents to the whole family of man, the question, whether a constitutional republic, or a democracy—a government of the peo- ple, by the same people—can, or cannot, maintain its territorial integrity, against its own domestic foes. It presents the question, whether discontented individuals, too few in numbers to control administration, according to organic law, in any case, can always, upon the pretences made in this case, or on any other pretences, or arbitrarily, without any pretence, break up their Government, and thus practically put an end to free government upon the earth. It forces us to ask: "Is there, in all republics, this inherent, and fatal weakness?" "Must a government, of necessity, be too *strong* for the liberties of its own people, or too *weak* to maintain its own existence?"...

It may be affirmed, without extravagance, that the free institutions we enjoy, have developed the powers, and improved the condition, of our whole people, beyond any example in the world. Of this we now have a striking, and an impressive illustration. So large an army as the government has now on foot, was never before known, without a soldier in it, but who had taken his place there, of his own free choice. But more than this: there are many single Regiments whose members, one and another, possess full practical knowledge of all the arts, sciences, professions, and whatever else, whether useful or elegant, is known in the world; and there is scarcely one, from which there could not be selected, a President, a Cabinet, a Congress, and perhaps a Court, abundantly competent to administer the government itself. Nor do I say this is not true, also, in the army of our late friends, now adversaries, in this contest; but if it is, so much better the reason why the government, which has conferred such benefits on both them and us, should not be broken up. Whoever, in any section, proposes to abandon such a government, would do well to consider, in deference to what principle it is, that he does it—what better he is likely to get in its stead—whether the substitute will give, or be in-

(*Continued on page 90*)

To my good friend, Mrs Fanny Speed.

A. Lincoln.

tended to give, so much of good to the people. There are some fore-shadowings on this subject. Our adversaries have adopted some Declarations of Independence; in which, unlike the good old one, penned by Jefferson, they omit the words "all men are created equal." Why? They have adopted a temporary national constitution, in the preamble of which, unlike our good old one, signed by Washington, they omit "We, the People," and substitute "We, the deputies of the sovereign and independent States." Why? Why this deliberate pressing out of view, the rights of men, and the authority of the people?

This is essentially a People's contest. On the side of the Union, it is a struggle for maintaining in the world, that form, and substance of government, whose leading object is, to elevate the condition of men—to lift artificial weights from all shoulders—to clear the paths of laudable pursuit for all—to afford all, an unfettered start, and a fair chance, in the race of life. Yielding to partial, and temporary departures, from necessity, this is the leading object of the government for whose existence we contend.

I am most happy to believe that the plain people understand, and appreciate this. It is worthy of note, that while in this, the government's hour of trial, large numbers of those in the Army and Navy, who have been favored with the offices, have resigned, and proved false to the hand which had pampered them, not one common soldier, or common sailor is known to have deserted his flag.

Great honor is due to those officers who remain true, despite the example of their treacherous associates; but the greatest honor, and most important fact of all, is the unanimous firmness of the common soldiers, and common sailors. To the last man, so far as known, they have successfully resisted the traitorous efforts of those, whose commands, but an hour before, they obeyed as absolute law. This is the patriotic instinct of the plain people. They understand, without an argument, that destroying the government, which was made by Washington, means no good to them.

Our popular government has often been called an experiment. Two points in it, our people have already settled—the successful *establishing*, and the successful *administering* of it. One still remains—its successful *maintenance* against a formidable [internal] attempt to overthrow it. It is now for them to demonstrate to the world, that those who can fairly carry an election, can also suppress a rebellion—that ballots are the rightful, and peaceful, successors of bullets; and that when ballots have fairly, and constitutionally, decided, there can be no successful appeal, back to bullets; that there can be no successful appeal, except to ballots themselves, at succeeding elections.

Such will be a great lesson of peace; teaching men that what they cannot take by an election, neither can they take it by a war—teaching all, the folly of being the beginners of a war.

Lest there be some uneasiness in the minds of candid men, as to what is to be the course of the government, towards the Southern States, *after* the rebellion shall have been suppressed, the Executive deems it proper to say, it will be his purpose then, as ever, to be guided by the Constitution, and the laws; and that he probably will have no different understanding of the powers, and duties of the Federal government, relatively to the rights of the States, and the people, under the Constitution, than that expressed in the inaugural address.

He desires to preserve the government, that it may be administered for all, as it was administered by the men who made it. Loyal citizens everywhere, have the right to claim this of their government; and the government has no right to withhold, or neglect it. It is not perceived that, in giving it, there is any coercion, any conquest, or any subjugation, in any just sense of those terms. . . .

It was with the deepest regret that the Executive found the duty of employing the war-power, in defence of the government, forced upon him. He could but perform this duty, or surrender the existence of the government. No compromise, by public servants, could, in this case, be a cure; not that compromises are not often proper, but that no popular government can long survive a marked precedent, that those who carry an election, can only save the government from immediate destruction, by giving up the main point, upon which the people gave the election. The people themselves, and not their servants, can safely reverse their own deliberate decisions. As a private citizen, the Executive could not have consented that these institutions shall perish; much less could he, in betrayal of so vast, and so sacred a trust, as these free people had confided to him. He felt that he had no moral right to shrink; nor even to count the chances of his own life, in what might follow. In full view of his great responsibility, he has, so far, done what he has deemed his duty. You will now, according to your own judgment, perform yours. He sincerely hopes that your views, and your action, may so accord with his, as to assure all faithful citizens, who have been disturbed in their rights, of a certain, and speedy restoration to them, under the Constitution, and the laws.

And having thus chosen our course, without guile, and with pure purpose, let us renew our trust in God, and go forward without fear, and with manly hearts.

From the President's message to Congress
in special session, July 4, 1861

Carte-de-visite printed from a lost contemporary negative
of one view of the multiple-image stereographic pose made by Alexander Gardner
at Mathew Brady's gallery, in Washington, D.C.,
about February 24, 1861. Mellon Collection.

Made from a lost copy negative of a lost retouched oval print, the carte-de-visite reproduced here is the only contemporary albumen print of this pose which is known to have survived. It is reproduced above in its actual size and at the right as an enlargement. Neither the photographer's identity nor the whereabouts of the original negative has been determined. However, the similarity between this portrait and the one which Lincoln autographed to Mrs. Fanny Speed (see page 89) is so obvious that the former was almost certainly made with the latter at a sitting known to have occurred between late February and the end of June 1861. This portrait and the aforementioned companion pose were made in Washington, D.C., and are probably the earliest known photographs of Lincoln as President of the United States. The two differ in the angle of Lincoln's head, which in this pose is turned more to the left, as seen from the distance between the tip of his nose and the profile of his left cheek. By superimposing film positives of the two poses, the compiler was able to determine with certainty that the facial lines of these portraits differ to an extent that neither the retouching nor a difference of stereo angle (if the original negatives of the two poses were stereographic plates) could have accounted for. Most important of all, the facial expression in the two poses is markedly different. While in the companion pose Lincoln has his usual thoughtful, slightly melancholy look, he appears to be on the verge of a smile in the pose reproduced here. On his right cheek can be seen the deeply-cleft dimple which gave such force to his smile, and the lines around his right eye are likewise puckered into an expression of incipient mirth.

The carte was acquired in 1967 by the Lincoln authority Lloyd Ostendorf from Roberta M. Guy, a schoolteacher in Richmond, Virginia. It is reproduced here by the kind permission of Mr. Ostendorf.

Lincoln's Strategy after the Union Defeat at Bull Run, July 1861

1. Let the plan for making the Blockade effective be pushed forward with all possible despatch.

2. Let the volunteer forces at Fort-Monroe & vicinity—under Genl. Butler—be constantly drilled, disciplined, and instructed without more for the present.

3. Let Baltimore be held, as now, with a gentle, but firm, and certain hand.

4. Let the force now under Patterson, or Banks, be strengthened, and made secure in its position.

5. Let the forces in Western Virginia act, till further orders, according to instructions, or orders from Gen. McClellan.

6. [Let] Gen. Fremont push forward his organization, and operations in the West as rapidly as possible, giving rather special attention to Missouri.

7. Let the forces late before Manassas, except the three months men, be reorganized as rapidly as possible, in their camps here and about Arlington.

8. Let the three months forces, who decline to enter the longer service, be discharged as rapidly as circumstances will permit.

9. Let the new volunteer forces be brought forward as fast as possible; and especially into the camps on the two sides of the river here.

When the foregoing shall have been substantially attended to—

1. Let Manassas junction (or some point on one or other of the railroads near it), and Strasburg, be seized, and permanently held, with an open line from Washington to Manassas, and open line from Harper's Ferry to Strasburg—the military men to find the way of doing these.

2. This done, a joint movement from Cairo on Memphis, and from Cincinnati on East Tennessee.

Memoranda, July 23 and 27, 1861; autograph document, unsigned

Lincoln Writes a Letter on the War

Cuthbert Bullitt Esq   Washington D.C.
New Orleans La.   July 28. 1862

Sir: The copy of a letter addressed to yourself by Mr. Thomas J. Durant, has been shown to me. The writer appears to be an able, a dispassionate, and an entirely sincere man. The first part of the letter is devoted to an effort to show that the Secession Ordinance of Louisiana was adopted against the will of a majority of the people. This is probably true; and in that fact may be found some instruction. Why did they allow the Ordinance to go into effect? Why did they not assert themselves? Why stand passive and allow themselves to be trodden down by a minority? Why did they not hold popular meetings, and have a convention of their own, to express and enforce the true sentiment of the state? If preorganization was against them *then*, why not do this *now*, that the United States Army is present to protect them? The paralysis—the dead palsy—of the government in this whole struggle is, that this class of men will do nothing for the government, nothing for themselves, except demanding that the government shall not strike its open enemies, lest they be struck by accident! . . .

I think I can perceive, in the freedom of trade, which Mr. Durant urges, that he would relieve both friends and enemies from the pressure of the blockade. By this he would serve the enemy more effectively than the enemy is able to serve himself. I do not say or believe that to serve the enemy is the purpose of Mr. Durant; or that he is conscious of any purpose, other than national and patriotic ones. Still, if there were a class of men who, having no choice of sides in the contest, were anxious only to have quiet and comfort for themselves while it rages, and to fall in with the victorious side at the end of it, without loss to themselves, their advice as to the mode of conducting the contest would be precisely such as his is. He speaks of no duty—apparently thinks of none—resting upon Union men. He even thinks it injurious to the Union cause that they should be restrained in trade and passage without taking sides. They are to touch neither a sail nor a pump, but to be merely passengers,—dead-heads at that—to be carried snug and dry, throughout the storm, and safely landed right side up. Nay, more; even a mutineer is to go untouched lest these sacred passengers receive an accidental wound.

Of course the rebellion will never be suppressed in Louisiana, if the professed Union men there will neither help to do it, nor permit the government to do it without their help.

Now, I think the true remedy is very different from what is suggested by Mr. Durant. It does not lie in rounding the rough angles of the war, but in removing the necessity for the war. The people of Louisiana who wish protection to person and property, have but to reach forth their hands and take it. Let them, in good faith, reinaugurate the national authority, and set up a State Government conforming thereto under the constitution. They know how to do it, and can have the protection of the Army while doing it. The Army will be withdrawn so soon as such State government can dispense with its presence; and the people of the State can then, upon the old Constitutional terms, govern themselves to their own liking. This is very simple and easy.

If they will not do this, if they prefer to hazard all for the sake of destroying the government, it is for them to consider whether it is probable I will surrender the government to save them from losing all. If they decline what I suggest, you scarcely need to ask what I will do. What would you do in my position? Would you drop the war where it is? Or, would you prosecute it in future, with elder-stalk squirts, charged with rose water? Would you deal lighter blows rather than heavier ones? Would you give up the contest, leaving any available means unapplied.

I am in no boastful mood. I shall not do *more* than I can, and I shall do *all* I can to save the government, which is my sworn duty as well as my personal inclination. I shall do nothing in malice. What I deal with is too vast for malicious dealing. Yours truly

A. LINCOLN

Carte-de-visite printed from one frame
of the lost original multiple-image stereographic negative
made by an unknown photographer at Mathew Brady's gallery, in Washington, D.C.,
about 1862. Courtesy of Set Momjian.

30

Encouraging Free Negroes to Volunteer for Colonization Abroad

. . . why should the people of your race be colonized, and where? Why should they leave this country? This is, perhaps, the first question for proper consideration. You and we are different races. We have between us a broader difference than exists between almost any other two races. Whether it is right or wrong I need not discuss, but this physical difference is a great disadvantage to us both, as I think your race suffer very greatly, many of them by living among us, while ours suffer from your presence. In a word we suffer on each side. If this is admitted, it affords a reason at least why we should be separated. You here are freemen I suppose.

A VOICE: Yes, sir.

The President: Perhaps you have long been free, or all your lives. Your race are suffering, in my judgment, the greatest wrong inflicted on any people. But even when you cease to be slaves, you are yet far removed from being placed on an equality with the white race. You are cut off from many of the advantages which the other race enjoy. The aspiration of men is to enjoy equality with the best when free, but on this broad continent, not a single man of your race is made the equal of a single man of ours. Go where you are treated the best, and the ban is still upon you.

I do not propose to discuss this, but to present it as a fact with which we have to deal. I cannot alter it if I would. It is a fact, about which we all think and feel alike, I and you. We look to our condition, owing to the existence of the two races on this continent. I need not recount to you the effects upon white men, growing out of the institution of Slavery. I believe in its general evil effects on the white race. See our present condition—the country engaged in war!—our white men cutting one another's throats, none knowing how far it will extend; and then consider what we know to be the truth. But for your race among us there could not be war, although many men engaged on either side do not care for you one way or the other. Nevertheless, I repeat, without the institution of Slavery and the colored race as a basis, the war could not have an existence.

It is better for us both, therefore, to be separated.

Address to a deputation of free negroes at the White House,
August 14, 1862

31

Three Fragments on the Trials of War

I am glad of this interview, and glad to know that I have your sympathy and prayers. We are indeed going through a great trial—a fiery trial. In the very responsible position in which I happen to be placed, being a humble instrument in the hands of our Heavenly Father, as I am, and as we all are, to work out his great purposes, I have desired that all my works and acts may be according to his will, and that it might be so, I have sought his aid—but if after endeavoring to do my best in the light which he affords me, I find my efforts fail, I must believe that for some purpose unknown to me, He wills it otherwise. If I had had my way, this war would never have been commenced; If I had been allowed my way this war would have been ended before this, but we find it still continues; and we must believe that He permits it for some wise purpose of his own, mysterious and unknown to us; and though with our limited understandings we may not be able to comprehend it, yet we cannot but believe, that he who made the world still governs it.

Reply to Eliza Gurney, October 26, 1862

Executive Mansion,
Washington, December 23, 1862.

Dear Fanny

    It is with deep grief that I learn of the death of your kind and brave Father; and, especially, that it is affecting your young heart beyond what is common in such cases. In this sad world of ours, sorrow comes to all; and, to the young, it comes with bitterest agony, because it takes them unawares. The older have learned to ever expect it. I am anxious to afford some alleviation of your present distress. Perfect relief is not possible, except with time. You can not now realize that you will ever feel better. Is not this so? And yet it is a mistake. You are sure to be happy again. To know this, which is certainly true, will make you some less miserable now. I have had experience enough to know what I say; and you need only to believe it, to feel better at once. The memory of your dear Father, instead of an agony, will yet be a sad sweet feeling in your heart, of a purer, and holier sort than you have known before.

    Please present my kind regards to your afflicted mother.

Your sincere friend   A. LINCOLN

Letter to twelve-year-old Fanny McCullough,
on the death of her father in battle

The will of God prevails. In great contests each party claims to act in accordance with the will of God. Both *may* be, and one *must* be wrong. God can not be *for,* and *against* the same thing at the same time. In the present civil war it is quite possible that God's purpose is something different from the purpose of either party—and yet the human instrumentalities, working just as they do, are of the best adaptation to effect His purpose. I am almost ready to say this is probably true—that God wills this contest, and wills that it shall not end yet. By his mere quiet power on the minds of the now contestants, He could have either *saved* or *destroyed* the Union without a human contest. Yet the contest began. And having begun, He could give the final victory to either side any day. Yet the contest proceeds.

Autograph document, unsigned, undated,
possibly September 2, 1862

Carte-de-visite printed from one frame
of the lost original multiple-image stereographic negative
made by an unknown photographer at Mathew Brady's gallery, in Washington, D.C.,
about 1862. Mellon Collection.

To Save the Union, with or without Slavery

Hon. Horace Greeley: Executive Mansion,
Dear Sir   Washington, August 22, 1862.

I have just read yours of the 19th. addressed to myself through the New-York Tribune. If there be in it
any statements, or assumptions of fact, which I may know to be erroneous, I do not, now and here, controvert
them. If there be in it any inferences which I may believe to be falsely drawn, I do not now and here, argue
against them. If there be perceptible in it an impatient and dictatorial tone, I waive it in deference to an old
friend, whose heart I have always supposed to be right.

As to the policy I "seem to be pursuing" as you say, I have not meant to leave any one in doubt.

I would save the Union. I would save it the shortest way under the Constitution. The sooner the national
authority can be restored, the nearer the Union will be "the Union as it was." If there be those who would
not save the Union unless they could at the same time *save* slavery, I do not agree with them. If there be
those who would not save the Union unless they could at the same time *destroy* slavery, I do not agree with
them. My paramount object in this struggle *is* to save the Union, and is *not* either to save or to destroy
slavery. If I could save the Union without freeing *any* slave I would do it, and if I could save it by freeing *all*
the slaves I would do it; and if I could save it by freeing some and leaving others alone I would also do that.
What I do about slavery, and the colored race, I do because I believe it helps to save the Union; and what I
forbear, I forbear because I do *not* believe it would help to save the Union. I shall do *less* whenever I shall
believe what I am doing hurts the cause, and I shall do *more* whenever I shall believe doing more will help
the cause. I shall try to correct errors when shown to be errors; and I shall adopt new views so fast as they
shall appear to be true views.

I have here stated my purpose according to my view of *official* duty; and I intend no modification of my
oft-expressed *personal* wish that all men every where could be free. Yours,

A. LINCOLN

Lincoln at the age of fifty-three.
Reproduced from a positive printed on film
from the original negative made by an unknown photographer
at Mathew Brady's gallery, in Washington, D.C.,
about 1862. National Archives.

The subject presented in the memorial is one upon which I have thought much for weeks past, and I may even say for months. I am approached with the most opposite opinions and advice, and that by religious men, who are equally certain that they represent the Divine will. I am sure that either the one or the other class is mistaken in that belief, and perhaps in some respects both. I hope it will not be irreverent for me to say that if it is probable that God would reveal his will to others, on a point so connected with my duty, it might be supposed he would reveal it directly to me; for, unless I am more deceived in myself than I often am, it is my earnest desire to know the will of Providence in this matter. *And if I can learn what it is I will do it!* These are not, however, the days of miracles, and I suppose it will be granted that I am not to expect a direct revelation. I must study the plain physical facts of the case, ascertain what is possible and learn what appears to be wise and right. The subject is difficult, and good men do not agree. For instance, the other day four gentlemen of standing and intelligence from New York called, as a delegation, on business connected with the war; but, before leaving, two of them earnestly beset me to proclaim general emancipation, upon which the other two at once attacked them! You know, also, that the last session of Congress had a decided majority of anti-slavery men, yet they could not unite on this policy. And the same is true of the religious people. Why, the rebel soldiers are praying with a great deal more earnestness, I fear, than our own troops, and expecting God to favor their side; for one of our soldiers, who had been taken prisoner, told Senator Wilson, a few days since, that he met with nothing so discouraging as the evident sincerity of those he was among in their prayers. But we will talk over the merits of the case.

What *good* would a proclamation of emancipation from me do, especially as we are now situated? I do not want to issue a document that the whole world will see must necessarily be inoperative, like the Pope's bull against the comet! Would *my word* free the slaves, when I cannot even enforce the Constitution in the rebel States? Is there a single court, or magistrate, or individual that would be influenced by it there? And what reason is there to think it would have any greater effect upon the slaves than the late law of Congress, which I approved, and which offers protection and freedom to the slaves of rebel masters who come within our lines? Yet I cannot learn that that law has caused a single slave to come over to us. And suppose they could be induced by a proclamation of freedom from me to throw themselves upon us, *what should we do with them?* How can we feed and care for such a multitude? Gen. Butler wrote me a few days since that he was issuing more rations to the slaves who have rushed to him than to all the white troops under his command. They *eat*, and that is all, though it is true Gen. Butler is feeding the whites also by the thousand; for it nearly amounts to a famine there. If, now, the pressure of the war should call off our forces from New Orleans to defend some other point, what is to prevent the masters from reducing the blacks to slavery again; for I am told that whenever the rebels take any black prisoners, free or slave, they immediately auction them off! They did so with those they took from a boat that was aground in the Tennessee river a few days ago. And then *I am very ungenerously attacked for it!* For instance, when, after the late battles at and near Bull Run, an expedition went out from Washington under a flag of truce to bury the dead and bring in the wounded, and the rebels seized the blacks who went along to help and sent them into slavery, Horace Greeley said in his paper that the Government would probably do nothing about it. What *could* I do? . . .

Reply to an emancipation memorial
presented by Chicago Christians of all denominations,
September 13, 1862

---

*Carte-de-visite printed from one frame
of the lost original multiple-image stereographic negative
made by an unknown photographer at Mathew Brady's gallery, in Washington, D.C.,
about 1862.* Meserve Collection.

A. Lincoln.

Lincoln's Vexation with General McClellan

Exasperated by the reluctance of Major General George B. McClellan to pursue and crush the defeated Confederate army after the pyrrhic Union victory at Antietam, Lincoln hastened from Washington to confer with his general face to face. The President's visit to the Army of the Potomac is recorded in the following five photographs taken for Mathew Brady by Alexander Gardner at McClellan's headquarters near Antietam, Maryland, October 3, 1862.

Major General McClellan   Executive Mansion,
My dear Sir   Washington, Oct. 13, 1862.

You remember my speaking to you of what I called your over-cautiousness. Are you not over-cautious when you assume that you can not do what the enemy is constantly doing? Should you not claim to be at least his equal in prowess, and act upon the claim?

As I understand, you telegraph Gen. Halleck that you can not subsist your army at Winchester unless the Railroad from Harper's Ferry to that point be put in working order. But the enemy does now subsist his army at Winchester at a distance nearly twice as great from railroad transportation as you would have to do without the railroad last named. He now wagons from Culpepper C.H. which is just about twice as far as you would have to do from Harper's Ferry. He is certainly not more than half as well provided with wagons as you are. I certainly should be pleased for you to have the advantage of the Railroad from Harper's Ferry to Winchester, but it wastes all the remainder of autumn to give it to you; and, in fact ignores the question of *time*, which can not, and must not be ignored.

Again, one of the standard maxims of war, as you know, is "to operate upon the enemy's communications as much as possible without exposing your own." You seem to act as if this applies *against* you, but can not apply in your *favor*. Change positions with the enemy, and think you not he would break your communication with Richmond within the next twentyfour hours? You dread his going into Pennsylvania. But if he does so in full force, he gives up his communications to you absolutely, and you have nothing to do but to follow, and ruin him; if he does so with less than full force, fall upon, and beat what is left behind all the easier.

Exclusive of the water line, you are now nearer Richmond than the enemy is by the route that you *can*, and he *must* take. Why can you not reach there before him, unless you admit that he is more than your equal on a march. His route is the arc of a circle, while yours is the chord. The roads are as good on yours as on his.

You know I desired, but did not order, you to cross the Potomac below, instead of above the Shenandoah and Blue Ridge. My idea was that this would at once menace the enemies' communications, which I would seize if he would permit. If he should move Northward I would follow him closely, holding his communications. If he should prevent our seizing his communications, and move towards Richmond, I would press closely to him, fight him if a favorable oppor-

tunity should present, and, at least, try to beat him to Richmond on the inside track. I say "try"; if we never try, we shall never succeed. If he make a stand at Winchester, moving neither North or South, I would fight him there, on the idea that if we can not beat him when he bears the wastage of coming to us, we never can when we bear the wastage of going to him. This proposition is a simple truth, and is too important to be lost sight of for a moment. In coming to us, he tenders us an advantage which we should not waive. We should not so operate as to merely drive him away. As we must beat him somewhere, or fail finally, we can do it, if at all, easier near to us, than far away. If we can not beat the enemy where he now is, we never can, he again being within the entrenchments of Richmond.

Recurring to the idea of going to Richmond on the inside track, the facility of supplying from the side away from the enemy is remarkable—as it were, by the different spokes of a wheel extending from the hub towards the rim—and this whether you move directly by the chord, or on the inside arc, hugging the Blue Ridge more closely. The chord-line, as you see, carries you by Aldie, Hay-Market, and Fredericksburg; and you see how turn-pikes, railroads, and finally, the Potomac by Acquia Creek, meet you at all points from Washington. The same, only the lines lengthened a little, if you press closer to the Blue Ridge part of the way. The gaps through the Blue Ridge I understand to be about the following distances from Harper's Ferry, to wit: Vestal's five miles; Gregorie's, thirteen, Snicker's eighteen, Ashby's twenty-eight, Manassas, thirty-eight, Chester forty-five, and Thornton's fifty-three. I should think it preferable to take the route nearest the enemy, disabling him to make an important move without your knowledge, and compelling him to keep his forces together, for dread of you. The gaps would enable you to attack if you should wish. For a great part of the way, you would be practically between the enemy and both Washington and Richmond, enabling us to spare you the greatest number of troops from here. When at length, running for Richmond ahead of him enables him to move this way; if he does so, turn and attack him in rear. But I think he should be engaged long before such point is reached. It is all easy if our troops march as well as the enemy; and it is unmanly to say they can not do it.

This letter is in no sense an order.

Yours truly   A. Lincoln

The President conferring with General McClellan.
Reproduced from a positive printed on film from the original negative.
Library of Congress.

Major Gen. McClellan.

Washington, D.C.,
July 2, 1862.

Your despatch of Tuesday morning induces me to hope your Army is having some rest. In this hope, allow me to reason with you a moment. When you ask for fifty thousand men to be promptly sent you, you surely labor under some gross mistake of fact. Recently you sent papers showing your disposal of forces, made last spring, for the defence of Washington, and advising a return to that plan. I find it included in, and about Washington seventyfive thousand men. Now please be assured, I have not men enough to fill that very plan by fifteen thousand. All of Fremont in the valley, all of Banks, all of McDowell, not with you, and all in Washington, taken together do not exceed, if they reach sixty thousand. With Wool and Dix added to those mentioned, I have not, outside of your Army, seventyfive thousand men East of the mountains. Thus, the idea of sending you fifty thousand, or any other considerable force promptly, is simply absurd. If in your frequent mention of responsibility, you have the impression that I blame you for not doing more than you can, please be relieved of such impression. I only beg that in like manner, you will not ask impossibilities of me. If you think you are not strong enough to take Richmond just now, I do not ask you to try just now. Save the Army, material and personal; and I will strengthen it for the offensive again, as fast as I can. The governors of eighteen states offer me a new levy of three hundred thousand, which I accept.

A. Lincoln

Majr. Genl. McClellan.

Washington City, D.C.
Oct. 24 [25]. 1862

I have just read your despatch about sore tongued and fatigued horses. Will you pardon me for asking what the horses of your army have done since the battle of Antietam that [could] fatigue anything?

A. Lincoln

Majr. Gen. McClellan.

Executive Mansion, Washington,
Oct. 27. 1862

Yours of yesterday received. Most certainly I intend no injustice to any; and if I have done any, I deeply regret it. To be told after more than five weeks total inaction of the Army, and during which period we had sent to that Army every fresh horse we possibly could, amounting in the whole to 7918 that the cavalry horses were too much fatigued to move, presented a very cheerless, almost hopeless, prospect for the future; and it may have forced something of impatience into my despatches. If not recruited, and rested then, when could they ever be? I suppose the river is rising, and I am glad to believe you are crossing.

A. Lincoln

The President and members of his party with General McClellan
and other officers. One frame of a stereographic card
printed from the lost original multiple-image negative. Mellon Collection.

(Left to right): *1. Captain David V. Derickson, a presidential bodyguard*
2. Ward H. Lamon, a friend of Lincoln's
3. The Honorable Ozias M. Hatch, Secretary of State for Illinois
4. Major General Randolph B. Marcy
5. Captain Wright Rives
6. Major General John A. McClernand
7. President Lincoln
8. Unidentified officer
9. Major General George B. McClellan
10. Joseph C. G. Kennedy, Superintendent of the Census
11. John W. Garrett, president of the Baltimore & Ohio Railroad
12. Colonel Thomas S. Mather

Lincoln charged that pompous General Butler "could strut sitting down"; that General Cass had once "*in*vaded Canada without resistance, and *out*vaded it without pursuit"; that General McClellan was "hollering" for so many reinforcements "they could not find room to lie down; they'd have to sleep standing up"; that General Frémont "was the damndest scoundrel that ever lived, but in the infinite mercy of Providence he was also the damndest fool"; that General Rosecrans was acting "like a duck hit on the head"; and that a particular Union army dwindled from desertions "like a shovelful of fleas pitched from one place to another."

Reproduced from a positive printed on film from the original negative.
Library of Congress. (*Detail on following pages.*)

(Left to right): *1. Colonel Delos B. Sacket*
2. Captain George Montieth
3. Lieutenant Colonel Nelson B. Sweitzer
4. Colonel George W. Morrell
5. Colonel Alexander S. Webb
6. Major General George B. McClellan
7. Adams (a scout)
8. Dr. Jonathan Letterman
9. Unidentified officer
10. President Lincoln
11. Brigadier General Henry J. Hunt
12. Major General Fitz-John Porter
13. Unidentified officer
14. Colonel Frederick T. Locke
15. Brigadier General Andrew A. Humphreys
16. Colonel George A. Batchelder

35

Lincoln Defends His Wartime Policy of Military Arrest
and Detention without Trial

Executive Mansion
Hon. Erastus Corning & others   Washington [June 12] 1863.

Gentlemen   Your letter of May 19th. inclosing the resolutions of a public meeting held at Albany, N.Y. on the 16th. of the same month, was received several days ago.

The resolutions, as I understand them, are resolvable into two propositions—first, the expression of a purpose to sustain the cause of the Union, to secure peace through victory, and to support the administration in every constitutional, and lawful measure to suppress the rebellion; and secondly, a declaration of censure upon the administration for supposed unconstitutional action such as the making of military arrests.

And, from the two propositions a third is deduced, which is, that the gentlemen composing the meeting are resolved on doing their part to maintain our common government and country, despite the folly or wickedness, as they may conceive, of any administration. This position is eminently patriotic, and as such, I thank the meeting, and congratulate the nation for it. My own purpose is the same; so that the meeting and myself have a common object, and can have no difference, except in the choice of means or measures, for effecting that object.

And here I ought to close this paper, and would close it, if there were no apprehension that more injurious consequences, than any merely personal to myself, might follow the censures systematically cast upon me for doing what, in my view of duty, I could not forbear. The resolutions promise to support me in every constitutional and lawful measure to suppress the rebellion; and I have not knowingly employed, nor shall knowingly employ, any other. But the meeting, by their resolutions, assert and argue, that certain military arrests and proceedings following them for which I am ultimately responsible, are unconstitutional. I think they are not. . . . Let us consider the real case with which we are dealing, and apply to it the parts of the constitution plainly made for such cases.

Prior to my installation here it had been inculcated that any State had a lawful right to secede from the national Union; and that it would be expedient to exercise the right, whenever the devotees of the doctrine should fail to elect a President to their own liking. I was elected contrary to their liking; and accordingly, so far as it was legally possible, they had taken seven states out of the Union, had seized many of the United States Forts, and had fired upon the United States' Flag, all before I was inaugurated; and, of course, before I had done any official act whatever. The rebellion, thus began soon ran into the present civil war; and, in certain respects, it began on very unequal terms between the parties. The insurgents had been preparing for it more than thirty years, while the government had taken no steps to resist them. The former had carefully considered all the means which could be turned to their account. It undoubtedly was a well pondered reliance with them that in their own unrestricted effort to destroy Union, constitution, and law, all together, the government would, in great degree, be restrained by the same constitution and law, from arresting their progress. Their sympathizers pervaded all departments of the government, and nearly all communities of the people. From this material, under cover of "Liberty of speech" "Liberty of the press" and *"Habeas corpus"* they hoped to keep on foot amongst us a most efficient corps of spies, informers, suppliers, and aiders and abettors of their cause in a thousand ways. They knew that in times such as they were inaugurating, by the constitution itself, the "Habeas corpus" might be suspended; but they also knew they had friends who would make a question as to *who* was to suspend it; meanwhile their spies and others might remain at large to help on their cause. Or if, as has happened, the executive should suspend the writ, without ruinous waste of time, instances of arresting innocent persons might occur, as are always likely to occur in such cases; and then a clamor could be raised in regard to this, which might be, at least, of some service to the insurgent cause. It needed no very keen perception to discover this part of the enemies' programme, so soon

(*Continued on page 118*)

"The imperial [-size] photograph, in which the head
leans upon the hand, I regard as the best that I have yet seen,"
wrote Lincoln in a note of thanks to the photographer.
Gelatin silver print of a lost contemporary albumen print
from the lost original negative made by Alexander Gardner,
in Washington, D.C., August 9, 1863. Ostendorf Collection.

Pages 114 and 115: *The President with Major General John A. McClernand*
and intelligence chief Allan Pinkerton. By swaying slightly during the exposures,
Lincoln blurred himself in both of these poses, reproduced here
from positives printed on film from the original negatives.
Library of Congress.

as by open hostilities their machinery was fairly put in motion. Yet, thoroughly imbued with a reverence for the guaranteed rights of individuals, I was slow to adopt the strong measures, which by degrees I have been forced to regard as being within the exceptions of the constitution, and as indispensable to the public Safety. Nothing is better known to history than that courts of justice are utterly incompetent to such cases. Civil courts are organized chiefly for trials of individuals, or, at most, a few individuals acting in concert; and this in quiet times, and on charges of crimes well defined in the law. Even in times of peace, bands of horse-thieves and robbers frequently grow too numerous and powerful for the ordinary courts of justice. But what comparison, in numbers, have such bands ever borne to the insurgent sympathizers even in many of the loyal states? Again, a jury too frequently have at least one member, more ready to hang the panel than to hang the traitor. And yet again, he who dissuades one man from volunteering, or induces one soldier to desert, weakens the Union cause as much as he who kills a union soldier in battle. Yet this dissuasion, or inducement, may be so conducted as to be no defined crime of which any civil court would take cognizance.

Ours is a case of Rebellion—so called by the resolutions before me—in fact, a clear, flagrant, and gigantic case of Rebellion; and the provision of the constitution that "The privilege of the writ of Habeas Corpus shall not be suspended, unless when in cases of Rebellion or Invasion, the public Safety may require it" is *the* provision which specially applies to our present case. This provision plainly attests the understanding of those who made the constitution that ordinary courts of justice are inadequate to "cases of Rebellion"— attests their purpose that in such cases, men may be held in custody whom the courts acting on ordinary rules, would discharge. Habeas Corpus, does not discharge men who are proved to be guilty of defined crime; and its suspension is allowed by the constitution on purpose that, men may be arrested and held, who can not be proved to be guilty of defined crime, "when, in cases of Rebellion or Invasion the public Safety may require it." This is precisely our present case—a case of Rebellion, wherein the public Safety does require the suspension. Indeed, arrests by process of courts, and arrests in cases of rebellion, do not proceed altogether upon the same basis. The former is directed at the small per centage of ordinary and continuous perpetration of crime; while the latter is directed at sudden and extensive uprisings against the government, which, at most, will succeed or

fail, in no great length of time. In the latter case, arrests are made, not so much for what has been done, as for what probably would be done. The latter is more for the preventive, and less for the vindictive, than the former. In such cases the purposes of men are much more easily understood, than in cases of ordinary crime. The man who stands by and says nothing, when the peril of his government is discussed, can not be misunderstood. If not hindered, he is sure to help the enemy. Much more, if he talks ambiguously—talks for his country with "buts" and "ifs" and "ands." Of how little value the constitutional provision I have quoted will be rendered, if arrests shall never be made until defined crimes shall have been committed, may be illustrated by a few notable examples. Gen. John C. Breckinridge, Gen. Robert E. Lee, Gen. Joseph E. Johnston, Gen. John B. Magruder, Gen. William B. Preston, Gen. Simon B. Buckner, and Commodore [Franklin] Buchanan, now occupying the very highest places in the rebel war service, were all within the power of the government since the rebellion began, and were nearly as well known to be traitors then as now. Unquestionably if we had seized and held them, the insurgent cause would be much weaker. But no one of them had then committed any crime defined in the law. Every one of them if arrested would have been discharged on Habeas Corpus, were the writ allowed to operate. In view of these and similar cases, I think the time not unlikely to come when I shall be blamed for having made too few arrests rather than too many.

By the third resolution the meeting indicate their opinion that military arrests may be constitutional in localities where rebellion actually exists; but that such arrests are unconstitutional in localities where rebellion, or insurrection, does not actually exist. They insist that such arrests shall not be made "outside of the lines of necessary military occupation, and the scenes of insurrection." Inasmuch, however, as the constitution itself makes no such distinction, I am unable to believe that there is any such constitutional distinction. I concede that the class of arrests complained of, can be constitutional only when, in cases of Rebellion or Invasion, the public Safety may require them; and I insist that in such cases, they are constitutional *wherever* the public safety does require them—as well in places to which they may prevent the rebellion extending, as in those where it may be already prevailing—as well where they may restrain mischievous interference with the raising and supplying of armies, to suppress the rebellion, as where the rebellion may actually be—as well where they may restrain the enticing men out of the army, as where they would prevent mutiny in the army—equally constitutional at all places where they will conduce to the public Safety, as against the dangers of Rebellion or Invasion.

Take the particular case mentioned by the meeting. They assert in substance that Mr. Vallandigham [a former member of the U.S. House of Representatives] was by a military commander, seized and tried "for no other reason than words addressed to a public meeting, in criticism of the course of the administration, and in condemnation of the military orders of that general." Now, if there be no mistake about this—if this assertion is the truth and the whole truth—if there was no other reason for the arrest, then I concede that the arrest was wrong. But the arrest, as I understand, was made for a very different reason. Mr. Vallandigham avows his hostility to the war on the part of the Union; and his arrest was made because he was laboring, with some effect, to prevent the raising of troops, to encourage desertions from the army, and to leave the rebellion without an adequate military force to suppress it. He was not arrested because he was damaging the political prospects of the administration, or the personal interests of the commanding general; but because he was damaging the army, upon the existence, and vigor of which, the life of the nation depends. He was warring upon the military; and this gave the military constitutional jurisdiction to lay hands upon him. If Mr. Vallandigham was not damaging the military power of the country, then his arrest was made on mistake of fact, which I would be glad to correct, on reasonably satisfactory evidence.

I understand the meeting, whose resolutions I am considering, to be in favor of suppressing the rebellion by military force—by armies. Long experience has shown that armies can not be maintained unless desertion shall be punished by the severe penalty of death. The case requires, and the law and the constitution, sanction this punishment. Must I shoot a simple-minded soldier boy who deserts, while I must not touch a hair of a wily agitator who induces him to desert? This is none the less injurious when effected by getting a father, or brother, or friend, into a public meeting, and there working upon his feelings, till he is persuaded to write the soldier boy, that he is fighting in a bad cause, for a wicked administration of a contemptible government, too weak to arrest and punish him if he shall desert. I think that in such a case, to silence the agitator, and save the boy, is not only constitutional, but, withal, a great mercy.

If I be wrong on this question of constitutional power, my error lies in believing that certain proceedings are constitutional when, in cases of rebellion or Invasion, the public Safety requires them, which would not be constitutional when, in absence of rebellion or invasion, the public Safety does not require them—in other words, that the constitution is not in its application in all respects the same, in cases of Rebellion or invasion, involving the public Safety, as it is in times of profound peace and public security. The constitution itself makes the distinction; and I can no more be persuaded that the government can constitutionally take no strong measure in time of rebellion, because it can be shown that the same could not be lawfully taken in time of peace, than I can be persuaded that a particular drug is not good medicine for a sick man, because it can be shown to not be good food for a well one. Nor am I able to appreciate the danger, apprehended by the meeting, that the American people will, by means of military arrests during the rebellion, lose the right of public discussion, the liberty of speech and the press, the law of evidence, trial by jury, and Habeas corpus, throughout the indefinite peaceful future which I trust lies before them, any more than I am able to believe that a man could contract so strong an appetite for emetics during temporary illness, as to persist in feeding upon them through the remainder of his healthful life.

In giving the resolutions that earnest consideration which you request of me, I can not overlook the fact that the meeting speak as "Democrats." Nor can I, with full respect for their known intelligence, and the fairly presumed deliberation with which they prepared their resolutions, be permitted to suppose that this occurred by accident, or in any way other than that they preferred to designate themselves "democrats" rather than "American citizens." In this time of national peril I would have preferred to meet you upon a level one step higher than any party platform; because I am sure that from such more elevated position, we could do better battle for the country we all love, than we possibly can from those lower ones, where from the force of habit, the prejudices of the past, and selfish hopes of the future, we are sure to expend much of our ingenuity and strength, in finding fault with, and aiming blows at each other. But since you have denied me this, I will yet be thankful, for the country's sake, that not all democrats have done so. He on whose discretionary judgment Mr. Vallandigham was arrested and tried, is a democrat, having no old party affinity with me; and the judge who rejected the constitu-

(*Continued on page 121*)

tional view expressed in these resolutions, by refusing to discharge Mr. V. on Habeas Corpus, is a democrat of better days than these, having received his judicial mantle at the hands of President Jackson. And still more, of all those democrats who are nobly exposing their lives and shedding their blood on the battle-field, I have learned that many approve the course taken with Mr. V. while I have not heard of a single one condemning it. I can not assert that there are none such.

And the name of President Jackson recalls a bit [an instance] of pertinent history. After the battle of New-Orleans, and while the fact that the treaty of peace had been concluded, was well known in the city, but before official knowledge of it had arrived, Gen. Jackson still maintained martial, or military law. Now, that it could be said the war was over, the clamor against martial law, which had existed from the first, grew more furious. Among other things a Mr. Louaillier published a denunciatory newspaper article. Gen. Jackson arrested him. A lawyer by the name of Morel procured the U.S. Judge Hall to order a writ of Habeas Corpus to release Mr. Louaillier. Gen. Jackson arrested both the lawyer and the judge. A Mr. Hollander ventured to say of some part of the matter that "it was a dirty trick." Gen. Jackson arrested him. When the officer undertook to serve the writ of Habeas Corpus, Gen. Jackson took it from him, and sent him away with a copy. Holding the judge in custody a few days, the general sent him beyond the limits of his encampment, and set him at liberty, with an order to remain till the ratification of peace should be regularly announced, or until the British should have left the Southern coast. A day or two more elapsed, the ratification of the treaty of peace was regularly announced, and the judge and others were fully liberated. A few days more, and the judge called Gen. Jackson into court and fined him a thousand dollars, for having arrested him and the others named. The general paid the fine, and there the matter rested for nearly thirty years, when congress refunded principal and interest. The late Senator Douglas, then in the House of Representatives, took a leading part in the debate, in which the constitutional question was much discussed. I am not prepared to say whom the Journals would show to have voted for the measure.

It may be remarked: First, that we had the same constitution then, as now. Secondly, that we then had a case of Invasion, and that now we have a case of Rebellion, and: Thirdly, that the permanent right of the people to public discussion, the liberty of speech and the press, the trial by jury, the law of evidence, and the Habeas Corpus, suffered no detriment whatever by that conduct of Gen. Jackson, or its subsequent approval by the American congress.

And yet, let me say that in my own discretion, I do not know whether I would have ordered the arrest of Mr. V. While I can not shift the responsibility from myself, I hold that, as a general rule, the commander in the field is the better judge of the necessity in any particular case. Of course I must practice a general directory and revisory power in the matter.

One of the resolutions expresses the opinion of the meeting that arbitrary arrests will have the effect to divide and distract those who should be united in suppressing the rebellion; and I am specifically called on to discharge Mr. Vallandigham. I regard this as, at least, a fair appeal to me, on the expediency of exercising a constitutional power which I think exists. In response to such appeal I have to say it gave me pain when I learned that Mr. V. had been arrested,—that is, I was pained that there should have seemed to be a necessity for arresting him—and that it will afford me great pleasure to discharge him so soon as I can, by any means, believe the public safety will not suffer by it. I further say that as the war progresses, it appears to me, opinion and action, which were in great confusion at first, take shape, and fall into more regular channels; so that the necessity for arbitrary [strong] dealing with them gradually decreases. I have every reason to desire that it would cease altogether; and far from the least is my regard for the opinions and wishes of those who, like the meeting at Albany, declare their purpose to sustain the government in every constitutional and lawful measure to suppress the rebellion. Still, I must continue to do so much as may seem to be required by the public safety.

A. LINCOLN

Carte-de-visite printed from a lost contemporary negative,
probably a copy, of one view of the multiple-image stereographic pose
made by Alexander Gardner, in Washington, D.C.,
August 9, 1863. Mellon Collection.

*Lincoln Offers the South Gradual, Voluntary Emancipation
with Compensation to Slave-Owners*

. . . I recommend the adoption of the following resolution and articles amendatory to the Constitution of the United States: . . .

"Article ——.

"Every State, wherein slavery now exists, which shall abolish the same therein, at any time, or times, before the first day of January, in the year of our Lord one thousand and nine hundred, shall receive compensation from the United States. . . .

"Article ——.

"All slaves who shall have enjoyed actual freedom by the chances of the war, at any time before the end of the rebellion, shall be forever free; but all owners of such, who shall not have been disloyal, shall be compensated for them, at the same rates as is provided for States adopting abolishment of slavery, but in such way, that no slave shall be twice accounted for.

"Article ——.

"Congress may appropriate money, and otherwise provide, for colonizing free colored persons, with their own consent, at any place or places without the United States." . . .

This plan is recommended as a means, not in exclusion of, but additional to, all others for restoring and preserving the national authority throughout the Union. The subject is presented exclusively in its economical aspect. The plan would, I am confident, secure peace more speedily, and maintain it more permanently, than can be done by force alone; while all it would cost, considering amounts, and manner of payment, and times of payment, would be easier paid than will be the additional cost of the war, if we rely solely upon force. It is much—very much—that it would cost no blood at all.

The plan is proposed as permanent constitutional law. It cannot become such without the concurrence of, first, two-thirds of Congress, and, afterwards, three-fourths of the States. The requisite three-fourths of the States will necessarily include seven of the Slave states. Their concurrence, if obtained, will give assurance of their severally adopting emancipation, at no very distant day, upon the new constitutional terms. This assurance would end the struggle now, and save the Union forever. . . .

Is it doubted, then, that the plan I propose, if adopted, would shorten the war, and thus lessen its expenditure of money and of blood? Is it doubted that it would restore the national authority and national prosperity, and perpetuate both indefinitely? Is it doubted that we here—Congress and Executive—can secure its adoption? Will not the good people respond to a united, and earnest appeal from us? Can we, can they, by any other means, so certainly, or so speedily, assure these vital objects? We can succeed only by concert. It is not "can *any* of us *imagine* better?" but "can we *all* do better?" Object whatsoever is possible, still the question recurs "can we do better?" The dogmas of the quiet past are inadequate to the stormy present. The occasion is piled high with difficulty, and we must rise with the occasion. As our case is new, so we must think anew, and act anew. We must disenthrall our selves, and then we shall save our country.

Fellow-citizens, *we* cannot escape history. We of this Congress and this administration, will be remembered in spite of ourselves. No personal significance, or insignificance, can spare one or another of us. The fiery trial through which we pass, will light us down, in honor or dishonor, to the latest generation. We *say* we are for the Union. The world will not forget that we say this. We know how to save the Union. The world knows we do know how to save it. We—even *we here*—hold the power, and bear the responsibility. In *giving* freedom to the *slave*, we *assure* freedom to the *free*—honorable alike in what we give, and what we preserve. We shall nobly save, or meanly lose, the last best hope of earth. Other means may succeed; this could not fail. The way is plain, peaceful, generous, just—a way which, if followed, the world will forever applaud, and God must forever bless.

From Lincoln's Second Annual Message to Congress,
December 1, 1862

Major General Joseph Hooker: Executive Mansion,
General. Washington, January 26, 1863.

I have placed you at the head of the Army of the Potomac. Of course I have done this upon what appear to me to be sufficient reasons. And yet I think it best for you to know that there are some things in regard to which, I am not quite satisfied with you. I believe you to be a brave and a skilful soldier, which, of course, I like. I also believe you do not mix politics with your profession, in which you are right. You have confidence in yourself, which is a valuable, if not an indispensable quality. You are ambitious, which, within reasonable bounds, does good rather than harm. But I think that during Gen. Burnside's command of the Army, you have taken counsel of your ambition, and thwarted him as much as you could, in which you did a great wrong to the country, and to a most meritorious and honorable brother officer. I have heard, in such way as to believe it, of your recently saying that both the Army and the Government needed a Dictator. Of course it was not *for* this, but in spite of it, that I have given you the command. Only those generals who gain successes, can set up dictators. What I now ask of you is military success, and I will risk the dictatorship. The government will support you to the utmost of its ability, which is neither more nor less than it has done and will do for all commanders. I much fear that the spirit which you have aided to infuse into the Army, of criticising their Commander, and withholding confidence from him, will now turn upon you. I shall assist you as far as I can, to put it down. Neither you, nor Napoleon, if he were alive again, could get any good out of an army, while such a spirit prevails in it.

And now, beware of rashness. Beware of rashness, but with energy, and sleepless vigilance, go forward, and give us victories. Yours very truly

A. LINCOLN

Washington, D.C.,
Major General Hooker June 5. 1863

Yours of to-day was received an hour ago. So much of professional military skill is requisite to answer it, that I have turned the task over to Gen. Halleck. He promises to perform it with his utmost care. I have but one idea which I think worth suggesting to you, and that is in case you find Lee coming to the North of the Rappahannock, I would by no means cross to the South of it. If he should leave a rear force at Fredericksburg, tempting you to fall upon it, it would fight in intrenchments, and have you at disadvantage, and so, man for man, worst you at that point, while his main force would in some way be getting an advantage of you Northward. In one word, I would not take any risk of being entangled upon the river, like an ox jumped half over a fence, and liable to be torn by dogs, front and rear, without a fair chance to gore one way or kick the other. If Lee would come to my side of the river, I would keep on the same side & fight him, or act on the defence, according as might be my estimate of his strength relatively to my own. But these are mere suggestions which I desire to be controlled by the judgement of yourself and Gen. Halleck.

A. LINCOLN

Contemporary albumen print believed to be the only surviving likeness
printed from the lost original negative, made by Alexander Gardner,
in Washington, D.C., August 9, 1863.
Courtesy of John Hay.

38

Nathaniel Hawthorne Meets "Uncle Abe"

By and by there was a little stir on the staircase and in the passage-way, and in lounged a tall, loose-jointed figure, of an exaggerated Yankee port and demeanor, whom (as being about the homeliest man I ever saw, yet by no means repulsive or disagreeable) it was impossible not to recognize as Uncle Abe.

Unquestionably, Western man though he be, and Kentuckian by birth, President Lincoln is the essential representative of all Yankees, and the veritable specimen, physically, of what the world seems determined to regard as our characteristic qualities. It is the strangest and yet the fittest thing in the jumble of human vicissitudes, that he, out of so many millions, unlooked for, unselected by any intelligible process that could be based upon his genuine qualities, unknown to those who chose him, and unsuspected of what endowments may adapt him for his tremendous responsibility, should have found the way open for him to fling his lank personality into the chair of state, —where, I presume, it was his first impulse to throw his legs on the council-table, and tell the Cabinet Ministers a story.

There is no describing his lengthy awkwardness, nor the uncouthness of his movement; and yet it seemed as if I had been in the habit of seeing him daily, and had shaken hands with him a thousand times in some village street; so true was he to the aspect of the pattern American, though with a certain extravagance which, possibly, I exaggerated still further by the delighted eagerness with which I took it in. If put to guess his calling and livelihood, I should have taken him for a country school-master as soon as anything else.

He was dressed in a rusty black frock coat and pantaloons, unbrushed, and worn so faithfully that the suit had adapted itself to the curves and angularities of his figure, and had grown to be an outer skin of the man. He had shabby slippers on his feet. His hair was black, still unmixed with gray, stiff, somewhat bushy, and had apparently been acquainted with neither brush nor comb that morning, after the disarrangement of the pillow; and as to a nightcap, Uncle Abe probably knows nothing of such effeminacies. His complexion is dark and sallow, betokening, I fear, an insalubrious atmosphere around the White House; he has thick black eyebrows and an impending brow; his nose is large, and the lines about his mouth are very strongly defined.

The whole physiognomy is as coarse a one as you would meet anywhere in the length and breadth of the States; but, withal, it is redeemed, illuminated, softened, and brightened by a kindly though serious look out of his eyes, and an expression of homely sagacity, that seems weighted with rich results of village experience.

A great deal of native sense; no bookish cultivation, no refinement; honest at heart, and thoroughly so, and yet, in some sort, sly, —at least, endowed with a sort of tact and wisdom that are akin to craft, and would impel him, I think, to take an antagonist in flank, rather than to make a bull-run at him right in front. But, on the whole, I like this sallow, queer, sagacious visage, with the homely human sympathies that warmed it; and, for my small share in the matter, would as lief have Uncle Abe for a ruler as any man whom it would have been practicable to put in his place.

The part of Hawthorne's interview with Lincoln (on March 13, 1862)
that *The Atlantic Monthly* refused to publish

I desire to so conduct the affairs of this Administration that if, at the end, when I come to lay down the reins of power, I have lost every other friend on earth, I shall at least have one friend left, and that friend shall be down inside of me.

Lincoln's remark to a visiting
delegation in 1863; cited in Ida M. Tarbell,
The Life of Abraham Lincoln

Contemporary albumen print from a lost negative
of one view of the defective multiple-image stereographic pose
made by Alexander Gardner, in Washington, D.C.,
August 9, 1863. Mellon Collection.

January 1, 1863

By the President of the United States of America:

A Proclamation.

Whereas, on the twenty-second day of September, in the year of our Lord one thousand eight hundred and sixty-two, a proclamation was issued by the President of the United States, containing, among other things, the following, towit:

"That on the first day of January, in the year of our Lord one thousand eight hundred and sixty-three, all persons held as slaves within any State or designated part of a State, the people whereof shall then be in rebellion against the United States, shall be then, thenceforward, and forever free; and the Executive Government of the United States, including the military and naval authority thereof, will recognize and maintain the freedom of such persons, and will do no act or acts to repress such persons, or any of them, in any efforts they may make for their actual freedom.

"That the Executive will, on the first day of January aforesaid, by proclamation, designate the States and parts of States, if any, in which the people thereof, respectively, shall then be in rebellion against the United States; and the fact that any State, or the people thereof, shall on that day be, in good faith, represented in the Congress of the United States by members chosen thereto at elections wherein a majority of the qualified voters of such State shall have participated, shall, in the absence of strong countervailing testimony, be deemed conclusive evidence that such State, and the people thereof, are not then in rebellion against the United States."

Now, therefore I, Abraham Lincoln, President of the United States, by virtue of the power in me vested as Commander-in-Chief, of the Army and Navy of the United States in time of actual armed rebellion against authority and government of the United States, and as a fit and necessary war measure for suppressing said rebellion, do, on this first day of January, in the year of our Lord one thousand eight hundred and sixty-three, and in accordance with my purpose so to do publicly proclaimed for the full period of one hundred days, from the day first above mentioned, order and designate as the States and parts of States wherein the people thereof respectively, are this day in rebellion against the United States, the following, towit:

Arkansas, Texas, Louisiana, (except the Parishes of St. Bernard, Plaquemines, Jefferson, St. Johns, St. Charles, St. James, Ascension, Assumption, Terrebonne, Lafourche, St. Mary, St. Martin, and Orleans, including the City of New-Orleans) Mississippi, Alabama, Florida, Georgia, South-Carolina, North-Carolina, and Virginia, (except the fortyeight counties designated as West Virginia, and also the counties of Berkley, Accomac, Northampton, Elizabeth-City, York, Princess Ann, and Norfolk, including the cities of Norfolk & Portsmouth); and which excepted parts are, for the present, left precisely as if this proclamation were not issued.

And by virtue of the power, and for the purpose aforesaid, I do order and declare that all persons held as slaves within said designated States, and parts of States, are, and henceforward shall be free; and that the Executive government of the United States, including the military and naval authorities thereof, will recognize and maintain the freedom of said persons.

And I hereby enjoin upon the people so declared to be free to abstain from all violence, unless in necessary self-defence; and I recommend to them that, in all cases when allowed, they labor faithfully for reasonable wages.

And I further declare and make known, that such persons of suitable condition, will be received into the armed service of the United States to garrison forts, positions, stations, and other places, and to man vessels of all sorts in said service.

And upon this act, sincerely believed to be an act of justice, warranted by the Constitution, upon military necessity, I invoke the considerate judgment of mankind, and the gracious favor of Almighty God.

In witness whereof, I have hereunto set my hand and caused the seal of the United States to be affixed.

Done at the City of Washington, this first day of January, in the year of our Lord one thousand eight hundred and sixty-three, and of the Independence of the United States of America the eighty-seventh.

By the President:

ABRAHAM LINCOLN

WILLIAM H. SEWARD, Secretary of State.

Gelatin silver print of Lincoln at the age of fifty-four, made by M. P. Rice in 1901 from the lost original negative made by Alexander Gardner, in Washington, D.C., August 9, 1863. Mellon Collection.

On the Use of Negro Troops and the Conduct of the War

Hon. James C. Conkling
My Dear Sir.

Executive Mansion,
Washington, August 26, 1863.

Your letter inviting me to attend a mass-meeting of unconditional Union-men, to be held at the Capital of Illinois, on the 3d day of September, has been received.

It would be very agreeable to me, to thus meet my old friends, at my own home; but I can not, just now, be absent from here, so long as a visit there would require.

The meeting is to be of all those who maintain unconditional devotion to the Union; and I am sure my old political friends will thank me for tendering, as I do, the nation's gratitude to those other noble men, whom no partisan malice, or partisan hope, can make false to the nation's life.

There are those who are dissatisfied with me. To such I would say: You desire peace; and you blame me that we do not have it. But how can we attain it? There are but three conceivable ways. First, to suppress the rebellion by force of arms. This, I am trying to do. Are you for it? If you are, so far we are agreed. If you are not for it, a second way is, to give up the Union. I am against this. Are you for it? If you are, you should say so plainly. If you are not for *force*, nor yet for *dissolution*, there only remains some imaginable *compromise*. I do not believe any compromise, embracing the maintenance of the Union, is now possible. All I learn, leads to a directly opposite belief. The strength of the rebellion, is its military—its army. That army dominates all the country, and all the people, within its range. Any offer of terms made by any man or men within that range, in opposition to that army, is simply nothing for the present; because such man or men, have no power whatever to enforce their side of a compromise, if one were made with them. To illustrate—Suppose refugees from the South, and peace men of the North, get together in convention, and frame and proclaim a compromise embracing a restoration of the Union; in what way can that compromise be used to keep Lee's army out of Pennsylvania? Meade's army can keep Lee's army out of Pennsylvania; and, I think, can ultimately drive it out of existence. But no paper compromise, to which the controllers of Lee's army are not agreed, can, at all, affect that army. In an effort at such compromise we should waste time, which the enemy would improve to our disadvantage; and that would be all. A compromise, to be effective, must be made either with those who control the rebel army, or with the people first liberated from the domination of that army, by the success of our own army. Now allow me to assure you, that no word or intimation, from that rebel army, or from any of the men controlling it, in relation to any peace compromise, has ever come to my knowledge or belief. All charges and insinuations to the contrary, are deceptive and groundless. And I promise you, that if any such proposition shall hereafter come, it shall not be rejected, and kept a secret from you. I freely acknowledge myself the servant of the people, according to the bond of service—the United States constitution; and that, as such, I am responsible to them.

But, to be plain, you are dissatisfied with me about the negro. Quite likely there is a difference of opinion between you and myself upon that subject. I certainly wish that all men could be free, while I suppose you do not. Yet I have neither adopted, nor proposed any measure, which is not consistent with even your view, provided you are for the Union. I suggested compensated emancipation; to which you replied you wished not to be taxed to buy negroes. But I had not asked you to be taxed to buy negroes, except in such way, as to save you from greater taxation to save the Union exclusively by other means.

You dislike the emancipation proclamation; and, perhaps, would have it retracted. You say it is unconstitutional—I think differently. I think the constitution invests its commander-in-chief with the law of war, in time of war. The most that can be said, if so much, is that slaves are property. Is there—has there ever been—any question that by the law of war, property, both of enemies and friends, may be taken when needed? And is it not needed whenever taking it, helps us, or hurts the enemy? Armies, the world over, destroy enemies' property when they can not use it; and even destroy their own to keep it from the enemy. Civilized belligerents do all in their power to help themselves, or hurt the enemy, except a few things regarded as barbarous or cruel. Among the exceptions are the massacre of vanquished foes, and non-combatants, male and female.

But the proclamation, as law, either is valid, or is not valid. If it is not valid, it needs no retraction. If it is valid, it can not be retracted, any more than the dead can be brought to life. Some of you profess to think its retraction would operate favorably for the Union. Why better *after* the retraction, than *before* the issue? There was more than a year and a half of trial to suppress the rebellion before the proclamation [was] issued, the last one hundred days of which passed under an explicit notice that it was coming, unless averted by those in revolt returning to their allegiance. The war has certainly progressed as favorably for us, since the issue of the proclamation as before. I know as fully as one can know the opinions of others, that some of the commanders of our armies in the field who have given us our most important successes, believe the emancipation policy, and the use of colored troops, constitute the heaviest blow yet dealt to the rebellion; and that, at least one of those important successes, could not have been achieved when it was, but for the aid of black soldiers. Among the commanders holding these views are some who have never had any affinity with what is called abolitionism, or with republican party politics; but who hold them purely as military opinions. I submit these opinions as being entitled to some weight against the objections, often urged, that emancipation, and arming the blacks, are unwise as military measures, and were not adopted, as such, in good faith.

You say you will not fight to free negroes. Some of them seem willing to fight for you; but, no matter. Fight you, then, exclusively to save the Union. I issued the proclamation on purpose to aid you in

(*Continued on page 132*)

Rare contemporary albumen print
from the lost original negative made by Alexander Gardner,
in Washington, D.C., November 8, 1863. Henry Ford Museum.

saving the Union. Whenever you shall have conquered all resistance to the Union, if I shall urge you to continue fighting, it will be an apt time, then, for you to declare you will not fight to free negroes.

I thought that in your struggle for the Union, to whatever extent the negroes should cease helping the enemy, to that extent it weakened the enemy in his resistance to you. Do you think differently? I thought that whatever negroes can be got to do as soldiers, leaves just so much less for white soldiers to do, in saving the Union. Does it appear otherwise to you? But negroes, like other people, act upon motives. Why should they do any thing for us, if we will do nothing for them? If they stake their lives for us, they must be prompted by the strongest motive—even the promise of freedom. And the promise being made, must be kept.

The signs look better. The Father of Waters again goes unvexed to the sea. Thanks to the great North-West for it. Nor yet wholly to them. Three hundred miles up, they met New-England, Empire, Key-Stone, and Jersey, hewing their way right and left. The Sunny South too, in more colors than one, also lent a hand. On the spot, their part of the history was jotted down in black and white. The job was a great national one; and let none be banned who bore an honorable part in it. And while those who have cleared the great river may well be proud, even that is not all. It is hard to say that anything has been more bravely, and well done, than at Antietam,

Murfreesboro, Gettysburg, and on many fields of lesser note. Nor must Uncle Sam's Web-feet be forgotten. At all the watery margins they have been present. Not only on the deep sea, the broad bay, and the rapid river, but also up the narrow muddy bayou, and wherever the ground was a little damp, they have been, and made their tracks. Thanks to all. For the great republic—for the principle it lives by, and keeps alive—for man's vast future,—thanks to all.

Peace does not appear so distant as it did. I hope it will come soon, and come to stay; and so come as to be worth the keeping in all future time. It will then have been proved that, among free men, there can be no successful appeal from the ballot to the bullet; and that they who take such appeal are sure to lose their case, and pay the cost. And then, there will be some black men who can remember that, with silent tongue, and clenched teeth, and steady eye, and well-poised bayonet, they have helped mankind on to this great consummation; while, I fear, there will be some white ones, unable to forget that, with malignant heart, and deceitful speech, they have strove to hinder it.

Still let us not be over-sanguine of speedy final triumph. Let us be quite sober. Let us diligently apply the means, never doubting that a just God, in his own good time, will give us the rightful result. Yours very truly

A. Lincoln

Suppose those now in rebellion should say: "We cease fighting: re-establish the national authority amongst us—customs, courts, mails, land-offices,—all as before the rebellion—we claiming to send members to both branches of Congress, as of yore, and to hold our slaves according to our State laws, notwithstanding anything, or all things, which has occurred during the rebellion." I probably should answer: "It will be difficult to justify in reason, or to maintain in fact, a war on one side, which shall have ceased on the other. You began the war, and you can end it. If questions remain, let them be solved by peaceful means—by courts, and votes. This war is an appeal, by you, from the ballot to the sword; and a great object with me has been to teach the futility of such appeal—to teach that what is decided by the ballot, can not be reversed by the sword—to teach that there can be no successful appeal from a fair election, but to the next election. Whether persons sent to congress, will be admitted to seats is, by the constitution, left to each House to decide, the President having nothing to do with it. Yet the question can not be one of indifference

to me. I shall dread, and I think we all should dread, to see 'the disturbing element' so brought back into the government, as to make probable a renewal of the terrible scenes through which we are now passing. During my continuance here, the government will return no person to slavery who is free according to the proclamation, or to any of the acts of congress, unless such return shall be held to be a legal duty, by the proper court of final resort, in which case I will promptly act as may then appear to be my personal duty."

Congress has left to me very large powers to remit forfeitures and personal penalties; and I should exercise these to the greatest extent which might seem consistent with the future public safety. I have thus told you, once more, so far as it is for me to say, what you are fighting for. The prospects of the Union have greatly improved recently; still, let us not be over-sanguine of a speedy final triumph. Let us diligently apply the means, never doubting that a just God, in his own good time, will give us the rightful result.

Autograph document, unsigned, undated,
about August 26, 1863

*Rare contemporary albumen print
from the lost original negative made by Alexander Gardner,
in Washington, D.C., November 8, 1863.* Brown University.

Overleaf, left and right: *Lincoln at the age of fifty-four.
Two rare contemporary albumen prints from the lost original negatives
made by Alexander Gardner, in Washington, D.C.,
November 8, 1863.* Mellon Collection.

41

The Gettysburg Address

Four score and seven years ago our fathers brought forth on this continent, a new nation, conceived in Liberty, and dedicated to the proposition that all men are created equal.

Now we are engaged in a great civil war, testing whether that nation, or any nation so conceived and so dedicated, can long endure. We are met on a great battle-field of that war. We have come to dedicate a portion of that field, as a final resting place for those who here gave their lives that that nation might live. It is altogether fitting and proper that we should do this.

But, in a larger sense, we can not dedicate—we can not consecrate—we can not hallow—this ground. The brave men, living and dead, who struggled here, have consecrated it, far above our poor power to add or detract. The world will little note, nor long remember what we say here, but it can never forget what they did here. It is for us the living, rather, to be dedicated here to the unfinished work which they who fought here have thus far so nobly advanced. It is rather for us to be here dedicated to the great task remaining before us—that from these honored dead we take increased devotion to that cause for which they gave the last full measure of devotion—that we here highly resolve that these dead shall not have died in vain—that this nation, under God, shall have a new birth of freedom—and that government of the people, by the people, for the people, shall not perish from the earth.

Delivered at the dedication of the cemetery at Gettysburg, Pennsylvania,
November 19, 1863

Lincoln, eleven days before delivering the Gettysburg Address.
Reproduced from a positive printed on film
from the cropped copy negative made by M. P. Rice, about 1890,
from a probable glass positive printed from the lost original negative
made by Alexander Gardner, in Washington, D.C.,
November 8, 1863. Ostendorf Collection.

Overleaf, left: *Only known photograph of Lincoln*
attending the ceremonies at Gettysburg, Pennsylvania, November 19, 1863.
The President is seated on the reviewing stand in this positive printed on film
from the original negative, made by an unknown photographer.
National Archives. (*Detail on pages 140–141.*)
Right: *Final text of the Gettysburg Address in*
Lincoln's handwriting. White House Collection.

Address delivered at the dedication of the Cemetery at Gettysburg.

Four score and seven years ago our fathers brought forth on this continent, a new nation, conceived in Liberty, and dedicated to the proposition that all men are created equal.

Now we are engaged in a great civil war, testing whether that nation, or any nation so conceived and so dedicated, can long endure. We are met on a great battle field of that war. We have come to dedicate a portion of that field, as a final resting place for those who here gave their lives, that that nation might live. It is altogether fitting and proper that we should do this.

But, in a larger sense, we can not dedicate— we can not consecrate— we can not hallow— this ground. The brave men, living and dead, who struggled here, have consecrated it, far above our poor power to add or detract. The world will little note, nor long remember what we say here, but it can never forget what they did here. It is for us the living, rather, to be dedicated here to the unfinished work which they who fought here have thus far so nobly advanced. It is rather for us to be here dedicated to the great task remaining before us— that from these honored dead we take increased devotion to that cause for which they gave the last full measure of devotion— that we here highly resolve that these dead shall not have died in vain— that this nation, under God, shall have a new birth of freedom— and that government of the people, by the people, for the people, shall not perish from the earth.

Abraham Lincoln.

November 19. 1863.

Legation of the United States, Paris, September 5, 1866
My dear Mr. Herndon:

. . . I will answer your questions as you put them without any attempt at arrangement.

Lincoln used to go to bed ordinarily from ten to eleven o'clock unless he happened to be kept up by important news, in which case he would frequently remain at the War Department until one or two. He rose early. When he lived in the country at Soldiers' Home, he would be up and dressed, eat his breakfast (which was extremely frugal—an egg, a piece of toast, coffee, etc.), and ride into Washington, all before eight o'clock. In the winter at the White House he was not quite so early. He did not sleep very well but spent a good while in bed. Tad usually slept with him. He would lie around the office until he fell asleep and Lincoln would shoulder him and take him off to bed.

He pretended to begin business at ten o'clock in the morning, but in reality the anterooms and halls were full before that hour— people anxious to get the first ax ground. He was extremely unmethodical: it was a four years' struggle on Nicolay's part and mine to get him to adopt some systematic rules. He would break through every regulation as fast as it was made.

Anything that kept the people themselves away from him he disapproved—although they nearly annoyed the life out of him by unreasonable complaints and requests.

He wrote very few letters. He did not read one in fifty that he received. At first we tried to bring them to his notice, but at last he gave the whole thing over to me, and signed without reading them the letters I wrote in his name. He wrote perhaps half a dozen a week himself, not more.

Nicolay received members of Congress, and other visitors who had business with the Executive Office, communicated to the Senate and House the messages of the President, and exercised a general supervision over the business.

I opened and read the letters, answered them, looked over the newspapers, supervised the clerks who kept the records, and in Nicolay's absence did his work also.

When the President had any rather delicate matter to manage at a distance from Washington, he very rarely wrote, but sent Nicolay or me.

The House remained full of people nearly all day. At noon the President took a little lunch—a biscuit, a glass of milk in winter, some fruit or grapes in summer. He dined at from five to six and we went off to our dinner also.

Before dinner was over, members and Senators would come back and take up the whole evening. Sometimes, though rarely, he shut himself up and would see no one. Sometimes he would run away to a lecture or concert or theater for the sake of a little rest.

He was very abstemious, ate less than anyone I know. Drank nothing but water, not from principle, but because he did not like wine or spirits. Once in rather dark days early in the war, a Temperance Committee came to him and said the reason we did not win was because our army drank so much whisky as to bring down the curse of the Lord upon them. He said dryly that it was rather unfair on the part of the aforesaid curse, as the other side drank more and worse whisky than ours did.

He read very little. Scarcely ever looked into a newspaper unless I called his attention to an article on some special subject. He frequently said: "I know more about that than any of them." It is absurd to call him a modest man. No great man was ever modest. It was his intellectual arrogance and unconscious assumption of superiority that men like Chase and Sumner never could forgive. . . .

I believe Lincoln is well understood by the people. Miss Nancy Bancroft and the rest of that patent-leather kid-glove set know no more of him than an owl does of a comet blazing into his blinking eyes. . . .

I consider Lincoln Republicanism incarnate, with all its faults and all its virtues. As, in spite of some evidences, Republicanism is the sole hope of a sick world, so Lincoln, with all his foibles, is the greatest character since Christ.

Yours,   JOHN HAY

"Nico & I immortalized ourselves
by having ourselves done in a group with the Prest.," exulted John Hay,
referring to this photograph of himself (right) and fellow secretary John Nicolay
with Lincoln. Contemporary albumen print from the lost original negative
made by Alexander Gardner, in Washington, D.C.,
November 8, 1863. Courtesy of George Rinhart.

43

On Reading and Shakespeare

Lincoln: "It may seem somewhat strange to say, but *I never read an entire novel in my life.*"
Judge:"Harris: Is it possible?"
Lincoln: "Yes, it is a fact. I once commenced *Ivanhoe*, but never finished it."

Cited in Francis Browne,
The Every-Day Life of Abraham Lincoln

I never read text books for I have no particular motive to drive and whip me to it. As I am constituted I don't love to read generally, and . . . I feel no interest in what is thus read. I don't, and can't remember such reading. When I have a particular case in hand I have that motive, and feel an interest in the case—feel an interest in ferreting out the questions to the bottom—love to dig up the question by the roots and hold it up and dry it before the fires of the mind. I know that general reading broadens the mind—makes it universal, but it never makes a precise deep clear mind. The study of particular cases does do that thing, as I understand it. General reading has its advantages and its disadvantages. Special case reading has its advantages and its disadvantages.

Lincoln, in conversation, to William Herndon;
cited in Herndon, "Analysis of the Character of Abraham Lincoln"

My dear Sir:

Executive Mansion,
Washington, August 17, 1863.

Months ago I should have acknowledged the receipt of your book, and accompanying kind note; and I now have to beg your pardon for not having done so.

For one of my age, I have seen very little of the drama. The first presentation of Falstaff I ever saw was yours here, last winter or spring. Perhaps the best compliment I can pay is to say, as I truly can, I am very anxious to see it again. Some of Shakspeare's plays I have never read; while others I have gone over perhaps as frequently as any unprofessional reader. Among the latter are Lear, Richard Third, Henry Eighth, Hamlet, and especially Macbeth. I think nothing equals Macbeth. It is wonderful. Unlike you gentlemen of the profession, I think the soliloquy in Hamlet commencing "O, my offence is rank" surpasses that commencing "To be, or not to be." But pardon this small attempt at criticism. I should like to hear you pronounce the opening speech of Richard the Third. Will you not soon visit Washington again? If you do, please call and let me make your personal acquaintance. Yours truly

A. LINCOLN

A letter to the distinguished Shakespearean actor James Hackett

*Detail of a contemporary albumen print
from the lost original negative, made by Alexander Gardner,
in Washington, D.C., November 8, 1863.* Mellon Collection.

44

Lincoln's Humor

A friend from Springfield: "Now, Mr. Lincoln, I want you to be honest with me and tell me how you like being President of the United States."
Lincoln: "You have heard the story, haven't you, about the man who was tarred and feathered and carried out of town on a rail? A man in the crowd asked him how he liked it. His reply was that if it was not for the honor of the thing, he would much rather walk."

Recalled by Lincoln's secretary William O. Stoddard;
cited in Emanuel Hertz, *Lincoln Talks*

The President last night had a dream.
He was in a party of plain people and as it became known who he was they began to comment on his appearance. One of them said, "He is a very common-looking man." The President replied, "Common-looking people are the best in the world: that is the reason the Lord makes so many of them."
Waking, he remembered it, and told it as rather a neat thing.

From the diary of Lincoln's secretary John Hay,
December 24, 1863

. . . A fellow . . . once came to me to ask for an appointment as minister abroad. Finding he could not get that, he came down to some more modest position. Finally he asked to be made a tide-waiter. When he saw he could not get that, he asked me for an old pair of trousers. But it is well to be humble.

Lincoln, in conversation, to Admiral David Porter; cited in Porter,
Incidents and Anecdotes of the Civil War

I laugh because I must not weep—that's all, that's all! (Sadly)

Lincoln; cited in H. C. Whitney,
Life on the Circuit

*Rare carte-de-visite printed from one frame of the
original multiple-image stereographic negative made by Lewis E. Walker,
in Washington, D.C., in 1863 or 1864. (This is an enlargement
of the image appearing on page 7.)* Mellon Collection.

Overleaf, left: *Carte-de-visite printed from one frame of
the lost original multiple-image stereographic negative;
(right) gelatin silver print of one view of a stereographic card
printed from two lower frames of the lost original multiple-image negative.
Both poses were made by Lewis E. Walker, in Washington, D.C., about 1864.*
Mellon Collection.

45

Lincoln in the White House

Soon afterwards there entered, with a shambling, loose, irregular, almost unsteady gait, a tall, lank, lean man, considerably over six feet in height, with stooping shoulders, long pendulous arms, terminating in hands of extraordinary dimensions, which, however, were far exceeded in proportion by his feet. He was dressed in an ill-fitting, wrinkled suit of black, which put one in mind of an undertaker's uniform at a funeral; round his neck a rope of black silk was knotted in a large bulb, with flying ends projecting beyond the collar of his coat; his turned-down shirt-collar disclosed a sinewy muscular yellow neck, and above that, nestling in a great black mass of hair, bristling and compact like a ruff of mourning pins, rose the strange quaint face and head, covered with its thatch of wild republican hair, of President Lincoln. The impression produced by the size of his extremities, and by his flapping and wide projecting ears, may be removed by the appearance of kindliness, sagacity, and the awkward bonhommie of his face; the mouth is absolutely prodigious; the lips, straggling and extending almost from one line of black beard to the other, are only kept in order by two deep furrows from the nostril to the chin; the nose itself—a prominent organ—stands out from the face with an inquiring, anxious air, as though it were sniffing for some good thing in the wind; the eyes dark, full, and deeply set, are penetrating, but full of an expression which almost amounts to tenderness; and above them projects the shaggy brow, running into the small hard frontal space, the development of which can scarcely be estimated accurately, owing to the irregular flocks of thick hair carelessly brushed across it. One would say that, although the mouth was made to enjoy a joke, it could also utter the severest sentence which the head could dictate, but that Mr. Lincoln would be ever more willing to temper justice with mercy, and to enjoy what he considers the amenities of life, than to take a harsh view of men's nature and of the world, and to estimate things in an ascetic or puritan spirit. A person who met Mr. Lincoln in the street would not take him to be what—according to the usages of European society—is called a "gentleman"; . . . but, at the same time, it would not be possible for the most indifferent observer to pass him in the street without notice.

William Howard Russell, war correspondent for *The Times* (London),
My Diary North and South

For myself, I feel—though the tax on my time is heavy—that no hours of my day are better employed than those which thus bring me again within the direct contact and atmosphere of the average of our whole people. Men moving only in an official circle are apt to become merely official—not to say arbitrary—in their ideas; and are apter and apter, with each passing day, to forget that they only hold power in a representative capacity. Now this is all wrong. I go into these promiscuous receptions of all who claim to have business with me twice each week, and every applicant for audience has to take his turn as if waiting to be shaved in a barber's shop. Many of the matters brought to my notice are utterly frivolous, but others are of more or less importance; and all serve to renew in me a clearer and more vivid image of that great popular assemblage out of which I sprang, and to which at the end of two years I must return . . . I call these receptions my public-opinion baths—for I have but little time to read the papers and gather public opinion that way; and, though they may not be pleasant in all their particulars, the effect as a whole is renovating and invigorating to my perceptions of responsibility and duty. It would never do for a President to have guards with drawn sabres at his door, as if he fancied he were, or were trying to be, or were assuming to be, an emperor.

Lincoln, in conversation, to Major Charles Halpine;
cited in Halpine, *Baked Meats of the Funeral*

*Gelatin silver print of a lost contemporary albumen print
from the lost original negative made by Anthony Berger at Mathew Brady's gallery,
in Washington, D.C., February 9, 1864. Library of Congress.*

46

"Just and Generous Sympathy"

The advice of a father to his son "Beware of entrance to a quarrel, but being in, bear it that the opposed may beware of thee," is good, and yet not the best. Quarrel not at all. No man resolved to make the most of himself, can spare time for personal contention. Still less can he afford to take all the consequences, including the vitiating of his temper, and the loss of self-control. Yield larger things to which you can show no more than equal right; and yield lesser ones, though clearly your own. Better give your path to a dog, than be bitten by him in contesting for the right. Even killing the dog would not cure the bite. . . .

From an autograph letter to James M. Cutts, Jr.,
unsigned, October 26, 1863

Mrs. Horace Mann
Madam,

Executive Mansion,
Washington, April 5, 1864

The petition of persons under eighteen, praying that I would free all slave children, and the heading of which petition it appears you wrote, was handed me a few days since by Senator Sumner. Please tell these little people I am very glad their young hearts are so full of just and generous sympathy, and that, while I have not the power to grant all they ask, I trust they will remember that God has, and that, as it seems, He wills to do it. Yours truly

A. LINCOLN

Executive Mansion, Washington,
Jan. 19, 1865.

Lieut. General Grant:

Please read and answer this letter as though I was not President, but only a friend. My son, now in his twenty second year, having graduated at Harvard, wishes to see something of the war before it ends. I do not wish to put him in the ranks, nor yet to give him a commission, to which those who have already served long, are better entitled, and better qualified to hold. Could he, without embarrassment to you, or detriment to the service, go into your Military family with some nominal rank, I, and not the public, furnishing his necessary means? If no, say so without the least hesitation, because I am anxious, and as deeply interested, that you shall not be encumbered as you can be yourself. Yours truly

A. LINCOLN

Contemporary albumen print of Lincoln and his son Tad,
from the lost original negative (believed to have been a multiple-image
stereographic plate) made by Anthony Berger at Mathew Brady's gallery,
in Washington, D.C., February 9, 1864. Ostendorf Collection.

47

Exhorting the People of Maryland to Approve the
Proposed Abolition of Slavery by State Law

The world has never had a good definition of the word liberty, and the American people, just now, are much in want of one. We all declare for liberty; but in using the same *word* we do not all mean the same *thing*. With some the word liberty may mean for each man to do as he pleases with himself, and the product of his labor; while with others the same word may mean for some men to do as they please with other men, and the product of other men's labor. Here are two, not only different, but incompatible things, called by the same name—liberty. And it follows that each of the things is, by the respective parties, called by two different and incompatible names—liberty and tyranny.

The shepherd drives the wolf from the sheep's throat, for which the sheep thanks the shepherd as a *liberator*, while the wolf denounces him for the same act as the destroyer of liberty, especially as the sheep was a black one. Plainly the sheep and the wolf are not agreed upon a definition of the word liberty; and precisely the same difference prevails to-day among us human creatures, even in the North, and all professing to love liberty. Hence we behold the processes by which thousands are daily passing from under the yoke of bondage, hailed by some as the advance of liberty, and bewailed by others as the destruction of all liberty. Recently, as it seems, the people of Maryland have been doing something to define liberty; and thanks to them that, in what they have done, the wolf's dictionary has been repudiated.

From an address at Baltimore, April 18, 1864

Understanding the spirit of our institutions to aim at the *elevation* of men;
I am opposed to whatever tends to degrade them.

From a letter to Theodore Canisius, May 17, 1859

Carte-de-visite printed from a lost contemporary negative
of a pose made by an unknown photographer, presumably in Washington, D.C.,
about 1864. Courtesy of Bruce Gimelson.

Groping for a Peaceful End to the War

Executive Mansion,

Sir: Washington, August 24. 1864.

You will proceed forthwith and obtain, if possible, a conference for peace with Hon. Jefferson Davis, or any person by him authorized for that purpose.

You will address him in entirely respectful terms, at all events, and in any that may be indispensable to secure the conference.

At said conference you will propose, on behalf [of] this government, that upon the restoration of the Union and the national authority, the war shall cease at once, all remaining questions to be left for adjustment by peaceful modes. If this be accepted, hostilities to cease at once.

If it be not accepted, you will then request to be informed what terms, if any, embracing the restoration of the Union, would be accepted. If any such be presented you in answer, you will forthwith report the same to this government, and await further instructions.

If the presentation of any terms embracing the restoration of the Union be declined, you will then request to be informed what terms of peace would be accepted; and on receiving any answer, report the same to this government, and await further instructions.

Autograph draft letter, unsigned, to Lincoln's friend Henry Raymond

---

*Reproduced from a positive printed on film
from the original negative made by Anthony Berger at Mathew Brady's gallery,
in Washington, D.C., February 9, 1864.* National Archives.

Overleaf, left and right: *Each of the two poses is
reproduced from a positive printed on film from a contemporary negative,
of one view of a multiple-image stereographic plate made by Mathew Brady,
in Washington, D.C., January 8, 1864.* National Archives.

While he was thus occupied [opening mail], I had an excellent opportunity of studying this extraordinary man. A marked change had taken place in his countenance since my first interview with him. He looked much older, and bore traces of having passed through months of painful anxiety and trouble. There was a sad, serious look in his eyes that spoke louder than words of the disappointments, trials, and discouragements he had encountered since the war began. The wrinkles about the eyes and forehead were deeper; the lips were firmer, but indicative of kindness and forbearance. The great struggle had brought out the hidden riches of his noble nature, and developed virtues and capacities which surprised his oldest and most intimate friends. He was simple but astute: he possessed the rare faculty of seeing things just as they are: he was a just, charitable, and honest man.

A. M. Ross, recalling a visit to the White House;
cited in Ross, *Recollections and Experiences of an Abolitionist*

He was in his plain two-horse barouche, and look'd very much worn and tired; the lines, indeed, of vast responsibilities, intricate questions, and demands of life and death, cut deeper than ever upon his dark brown face; yet all the old goodness, tenderness, sadness, and canny shrewdness, underneath the furrows. (I never see that man without feeling that he is one to become personally attach'd to, for his combination of purest, heartiest tenderness, and native western form of manliness.) By his side sat his little boy, of ten years. There were no soldiers, only a lot of civilians on horseback with huge yellow scarfs over their shoulders, riding around the carriage. . . . They pass'd me once very close, and I saw the President in the face fully, as they were moving slowly, and his look, though abstracted, happen'd to be directed steadily in my eye. He bow'd and smiled, but far beneath his smile I noticed well the expression I have alluded to. None of the artists or pictures has caught the deep, though subtle and indirect expression of this man's face. There is something else there. One of the great portrait painters of two or three centuries ago is needed.

Walt Whitman, on seeing the President
in Washington, D.C., during the war, *Autobiographia*

*The pose of the fifty-five-year-old Lincoln
from which the image on the five-dollar bill was engraved.
Contemporary albumen print made for Secretary of State Seward from the
original negative made by Anthony Berger
at Mathew Brady's gallery, in Washington, D.C., February 9, 1864.*
Mellon Collection.

Page 160: *Carte-de-visite
printed from one frame of the lost original multiple-image
stereographic negative.* Mellon Collection.
Page 161: *Reproduced from a positive
printed on film from a contemporary negative of one
view of the multiple-image stereographic pose.* National Archives.
*Both poses made by Mathew Brady, in Washington, D.C.,
January 8, 1864.*

50

Lincoln Explains His Reluctance to Withdraw
from the Presidential Race of 1864

They urge me with almost violent language to withdraw from the contest, although I have been unanimously nominated, in order to make room for a better man. I wish I could. Perhaps some other man might do this business better than I. That is possible. I do not deny it. But I am here, and that better man is not here. And if I should step aside to make room for him, it is not at all sure—perhaps not even probable—that he would get here. It is much more likely that the factions opposed to me would fall to fighting among themselves, and that those who want me to make room for a better man would get a man whom most of them would not want in at all. My withdrawal, therefore, might, and probably would, bring on a confusion worse confounded. God knows, I have at least tried very hard to do my duty—to do right to everybody and wrong to nobody. And now to have it said by men who have been my friends and who ought to know me better, that I have been seduced by what they call the lust of power, and that I have been doing this and that unscrupulous thing hurtful to the common cause, only to keep myself in office! Have they thought of that common cause when trying to break me down? I hope they have. . . . Well, things might look better, and they might look worse. . . . let us all do the best we can.

Recalled by Major General Carl Schurz,
The Reminiscences of Carl Schurz

Reproduced from a positive printed on film
from a contemporary negative of one view of the multiple-image
stereographic pose made by Anthony Berger at Mathew Brady's gallery,
in Washington, D.C., February 9, 1864. National Archives.

On Being Re-Elected President

It has long been a grave question whether any government, not *too* strong for the liberties of its people, can be strong *enough* to maintain its own existence, in great emergencies.

On this point the present rebellion brought our republic to a severe test; and a presidential election occurring in regular course during the rebellion added not a little to the strain. If the loyal people, *united*, were put to the utmost of their strength by the rebellion, must they not fail when *divided*, and partially paralyzed, by a political war among themselves?

But the election was a necessity.

We can not have free government without elections; and if the rebellion could force us to forego, or postpone a national election, it might fairly claim to have already conquered and ruined us. The strife of the election is but human-nature practically applied to the facts of the case. What has occurred in this case, must ever recur in similar cases. Human-nature will not change. In any future great national trial, compared with the men of this, we shall have as weak, and as strong; as silly and as wise; as bad and good. Let us, therefore, study the incidents of this, as philosophy to learn wisdom from, and none of them as wrongs to be revenged.

But the election, along with its incidental, and undesirable strife, has done good too. It has demonstrated that a people's government can sustain a national election, in the midst of a great civil war. Until now it has not been known to the world that this was a possibility. It shows also how *sound*, and how *strong* we still are. It shows that, even among candidates of the same party, he who is most devoted to the Union, and most opposed to treason, can receive most of the people's votes. It shows also, to the extent yet known, that we have more men now, than we had when the war began. Gold is good in its place; but living, brave, patriotic men, are better than gold.

But the rebellion continues; and now that the election is over, may not all, having a common interest, re-unite in a common effort, to save our common country? For my own part I have striven, and shall strive to avoid placing any obstacle in the way. So long as I have been here I have not willingly planted a thorn in any man's bosom.

While I am deeply sensible to the high compliment of a re-election; and duly grateful, as I trust, to Almighty God for having directed my countrymen to a right conclusion, as I think, for their own good, it adds nothing to my satisfaction that any other man may be disappointed or pained by the result.

May I ask those who have not differed with me, to join with me, in this same spirit towards those who have?

And now, let me close by asking three hearty cheers for our brave soldiers and seamen and their gallant and skilful commanders.

Response to a serenade at the White House,
November 10, 1864; autograph document, unsigned

Executive Mansion, Washington,
Dec. 26, 1864.

My dear General Sherman.

Many, many, thanks for your Christmas-gift—the capture of Savannah.

When you were about leaving Atlanta for the Atlantic coast, I was *anxious*, if not fearful; but feeling that you were the better judge, and remembering that "nothing risked, nothing gained" I did not interfere. Now, the undertaking being a success, the honor is all yours; for I believe none of us went farther than to acquiesce. And, taking the work of Gen. Thomas into the count, as it should be taken, it is indeed a great success. Not only does it afford the obvious and immediate military advantages; but, in showing to the world that your army could be divided, putting the stronger part to an important new service, and yet leaving enough to vanquish the old opposing force of the whole—Hood's army—it brings those who sat in darkness, to see a great light. But what next? I suppose it will be safer if I leave Gen. Grant and yourself to decide.

Please make my grateful acknowledgments to your whole army, officers and men. Yours very truly

A. LINCOLN

Executive Mansion,
Washington, Nov. 21, 1864.

Dear Madam,—I have been shown in the files of the War Department a statement of the Adjutant General of Massachusetts that you are the mother of five sons who have died gloriously on the field of battle.

I feel how weak and fruitless must be any words of mine which should attempt to beguile you from the grief of a loss so overwhelming. But I cannot refrain from tendering to you the consolation that may be found in the thanks of the Republic they died to save.

I pray that our Heavenly Father may assuage the anguish of your bereavement, and leave you only the cherished memory of the loved and lost, and the solemn pride that must be yours, to have laid so costly a sacrifice upon the altar of Freedom. Yours, very sincerely and respectfully,

Mrs. Bixby.

A. LINCOLN

Cypher.
Lieut. Genl. Grant
City-Point, Va.

Office U.S. Military Telegraph,
War Department,
Washington, D.C., August 3, 1864.

I have seen your despatch in which you say "I want Sheridan put in command of all the troops in the field, with instructions to put himself South of the enemy, and follow him to the death. Wherever the enemy goes, let our troops go also." This, I think, is exactly right, as to how our forces should move. But please look over the despatches you may have received from here, even since you made that order, and discover, if you can, that there is any idea in the head of any one here, of "putting our army *South* of the enemy" or of "following him to the *death*" in any direction. I repeat to you it will neither be done nor attempted unless you watch it every day, and hour, and force it.

A. LINCOLN

Reproduced from a positive printed on film from the original negative
made for the portrait painter Francis Carpenter
by Anthony Berger at Mathew Brady's gallery, in Washington, D.C.,
April 20, 1864. Ostendorf Collection.

You desire to know, in the event of our complete success in the field, the same being followed by a loyal and cheerful submission on the part of the South, if universal amnesty should not be accompanied with universal suffrage.

Now, since you know my private inclinations as to what terms should be granted to the South in the contingency mentioned, I will here add, that if our success should thus be realized, followed by such desired results, I cannot see, if universal amnesty is granted, how, under the circumstances, I can avoid exacting in return universal suffrage, or, at least, suffrage on the basis of intelligence and military service.

How to better the condition of the colored race has long been a study which has attracted my serious and careful attention; hence I think I am clear and decided as to what course I shall pursue in the premises, regarding it a religious duty, as the nation's guardian of these people, who have so heroically vindicated their manhood on the battle-field, where, in assisting to save the life of the Republic, they have demonstrated in blood their right to the ballot, which is but the humane protection of the flag they have so fearlessly defended.

The restoration of the Rebel States to the Union must rest upon the principle of civil and political equality of both races; and it must be sealed by general amnesty.

Newspaper account of a lost letter from
President Lincoln to Major General James S. Wadsworth,
undated, about January 1864

FELLOW CITIZENS:....There are but few aspects of this great war on which I have not already expressed my views by speaking or writing. There is one—the recent effort of our erring bretheren, sometimes so-called, to employ the slaves in their armies. The great question with them has been; "will the negro fight for them?" They ought to know better than we; and, doubtless, do know better than we. I may incidentally remark, however, that having, in my life, heard many arguments,—or strings of words meant to pass for arguments,—intended to show that the negro ought to be a slave, that if he shall now really fight to keep himself a slave, it will be a far better argument why he should remain a slave than I have ever before heard. He, perhaps, ought to be a slave, if he desires it ardently enough to fight for it. Or, if one out of four will, for his own freedom, fight to keep the other three in slavery, he ought to be a slave for his selfish meanness. I have always thought that all men should be free; but if any should be slaves it should be first those who desire it for *themselves*, and secondly those who *desire* it for *others*. Whenever I hear any one arguing for slavery I feel a strong impulse to see it tried on him personally.

There is one thing about the negroes fighting for the rebels which we can know as well as they can; and that is that they can not, at the same time fight in their armies, and stay at home and make bread for them. And this being known and remembered we can have but little concern whether they become soldiers or not. I am rather in favor of the measure; and would at any time if I could, have loaned them a vote to carry it. We have to reach the bottom of the insurgent resources; and that they employ, or seriously think of employing, the slaves as soldiers, gives us glimpses of the bottom. Therefore I am glad of what we learn on this subject.

From a speech to the 140th Indiana Regiment,
March 17, 1865

Lincoln, beside the table at which he signed the Emancipation Proclamation.
Gelatin silver print of a lost contemporary albumen print
from the lost original negative made at the White House for the portrait painter
Francis Carpenter by Anthony Berger of Mathew Brady's gallery,
April 26, 1864. Meserve Collection.

54

An Army Officer Confronts Lincoln with the Possibility of Assassination

. . . I had very frequently called the attention both of Major Hay and General Halleck [to] the utterly unprotected condition of the President's person, and the fact that any assassin or maniac, seeking his life, could enter his presence without the interference of a single armed man to hold him back. The entrance-doors, and all doors on the official side of the building, were open at all hours of the day and very late into the evening; and I have many times entered the mansion and walked up to the rooms of the two private secretaries, as late as nine or ten o'clock at night, without seeing or being challenged by a single soul. There were, indeed, two attendants—one for the outer door, and the other for the door of the official chambers; but these, thinking, I suppose, that none would call after office-hours save persons who were personally acquainted, or had the right of official entry—were, not unfrequently, somewhat remiss in their duties.

To this fact I now ventured to call the President's attention, saying that to me—perhaps from my European education—it appeared a deliberate courting of danger, even if the country were in a state of the profoundest peace, for the person at the head of the nation to remain so unprotected.

"Even granting, Mr. Lincoln," I said, "that no assassin should seek your life, the large number of lunatics always in a community, and always larger in times like these, and the tendency which insanity has to strike at shining objects, or whomsoever is most talked about, should lead—I submit—to some guards about the place, and to some permanent officers with the power and duty of questioning all who seek to enter. . . .

"There are two dangers, therefore," I wound up by saying; "the danger of deliberate political assassination, and the mere brute violence of insanity."

Mr. Lincoln had heard me with a smile, his hands still locked across his knees, and his body still rocking back and forth—the common indication that he was amused.

"Now, as to political assassination," he said, "do you think the Richmond people would like to have [Vice President] Hannibal Hamlin here any better than myself? In that one alternative, I have an insurance on my life worth half the prairie-land of Illinois. And besides"—this more gravely—"if there were such a plot, and they wanted to get at me, no vigilance could keep them out. We are so mixed up in our affairs, that—no matter what the system established—a conspiracy to assassinate, if such there were, could easily obtain a pass to see me for any one or more of its instruments. To betray fear of this, by placing guards, and so forth, would only be to put the idea into their heads, and perhaps lead to the very result it was intended to prevent. As to the crazy folks, Major, why I must only take my chances—the worst crazy people I at present fear being some of my own too zealous adherents. That there may be such dangers as you and many others have suggested to me, is quite possible; but I guess it wouldn't improve things any, to publish that we were afraid of them in advance."

Conversation between the President and
Major Charles Halpine during the war;
cited in Halpine, *Baked Meats of the Funeral*

*One of the two poses of the fifty-five-year-old President that inspired
the image on the one-cent piece (see also page 199, upper left).
Reproduced from a positive printed on film from one frame
of the original multiple-image stereographic negative made by Anthony Berger
at Mathew Brady's gallery, in Washington, D.C.,
February 9, 1864.* Meserve Collection.

*Overleaf, left: Carte-de-visite printed from one frame
of the lost original multiple-image stereographic negative.*
Right: *Gelatin silver print of a carte-de-visite printed from one frame
of the lost original multiple-image stereographic negative. Both poses
made by Alexander Gardner, in Washington, D.C., between
early February and mid-April 1865.* Mellon Collection.

ABRAHAM LINCOLN, Pres't U. S.

Entered according to Act of Congress, by Alex. Gardner, in the year 1865, in
the Clerk's Office of the District Court for the District of Columbia.

December 8, 1863

By the President of the United States of America:

A Proclamation

Whereas, in and by the Constitution of the United States, it is provided that the President "shall have power to grant reprieves and pardons for offences against the United States, except in cases of impeachment"; and

Whereas a rebellion now exists whereby the loyal State governments of several States have for a long time been subverted, and many persons have committed and are now guilty of treason against the United States; and . . .

Whereas it is now desired by some persons heretofore engaged in said rebellion to resume their allegiance to the United States, and to reinaugurate loyal State governments within and for their respective States; therefore,

I, Abraham Lincoln, President of the United States, do proclaim, declare, and make known to all persons who have, directly or by implication, participated in the existing rebellion, except as hereinafter excepted, that a full pardon is hereby granted to them and each of them, with restoration of all rights of property, except as to slaves, and in property cases where rights of third parties shall have intervened, and upon the condition that every such person shall take and subscribe an oath, and thenceforward keep and maintain said oath inviolate; and which oath shall be registered for permanent preservation, and shall be of the tenor and effect following, to wit:

"I, ———, do solemnly swear, in presence of Almighty God, that I will henceforth faithfully support, protect and defend the Constitution of the United States, and the union of the States thereunder; and that I will, in like manner, abide by and faithfully support all acts of Congress passed during the existing rebellion with reference to slaves, so long and so far as not repealed, modified or held void by Congress, or by decision of the Supreme Court; and that I will, in like manner, abide by and faithfully support all proclamations of the President made during the existing rebellion having reference to slaves, so long and so far as not modified or declared void by decision of the Supreme Court. So help me God."

The persons excepted from the benefits of the foregoing provisions are all who are, or shall have been, civil or diplomatic officers or agents of the so-called confederate government; all who have left judicial stations under the United States to aid the rebellion; all who are, or shall have been, military or naval officers of said so-called confederate government above the rank of colonel in the army, or of lieutenant in the navy; all who left seats in the United States Congress to aid the rebellion; all who resigned commissions in the army or navy of the United States, and afterwards aided the rebellion; and all who have engaged in any way in treating colored persons or white persons, in charge of such, otherwise than lawfully as prisoners of war, and which persons may have been found in the United States service, as soldiers, seamen, or in any other capacity.

And I do further proclaim, declare, and make known, that whenever, in any of the States of Arkansas, Texas, Louisiana, Mississippi, Tennessee, Alabama, Georgia, Florida, South Carolina, and North Carolina, a number of persons, not less than one-tenth in number of the votes cast in such State at the Presidential election of the year of our Lord one thousand eight hundred and sixty, each having taken the oath aforesaid and not having since violated it, and being a qualified voter by the election law of the State existing immediately before the so-called act of secession, and excluding all others, shall re-establish a State government which shall be republican, and in no wise contravening said oath, such shall be recognized as the true government of the State, and the State shall receive thereunder the benefits of the constitutional provision which declares that "The United States shall guaranty to every State in this union a republican form of government, and shall protect each of them against invasion; and, on application of the legislature, or the executive, (when the legislature cannot be convened,) against domestic violence."

And I do further proclaim, declare, and make known that any provision which may be adopted by such State government in relation to the freed people of such State, which shall recognize and declare their permanent freedom, provide for their education, and which may yet be consistent, as a temporary arrangement, with their present condition as a laboring, landless, and homeless class, will not be objected to by the national Executive.

. . . this proclamation is intended to present the people of the States wherein the national authority has been suspended, and loyal State governments have been subverted, a mode in and by which the national authority and loyal State governments may be re-established within said States, or in any of them; and, while the mode presented is the best the Executive can suggest, with his present impressions, it must not be understood that no other possible mode would be acceptable.

Given under my hand at the city, of Washington, the 8th. day of December, A. D. one thousand eight hundred and sixty-three, and of the independence of the United States of America the eighty-eighth.

ABRAHAM LINCOLN

By the President:

WILLIAM H. SEWARD, Secretary of State

Lincoln with his son Tad. Gelatin silver print
of a lost contemporary albumen print from the lost original negative
made by Alexander Gardner, in Washington, D.C., between
early February and mid-April 1865. Library of Congress.

Overleaf, left and right: *Two rare unretouched*
cartes-de-visite printed from the lost original negatives
of the two known poses made by Henry F. Warren on the White House balcony,
March 6, 1865. Ostendorf Collection.

PRESIDENT LINCOLN.

Photographed on the Balcony at the White House,
March 6, 1865, by

WARREN,   WALTHAM.

H. F. WARREN, PHO.,   WALTHAM, MASS.

PRESIDENT LINCOLN.

Pho. on the Balcony at the White House, March 6, 1865.

Lincoln delivering his second inaugural address, March 4, 1865.
Contemporary albumen print made from the lost original negative
by Alexander Gardner. Courtesy of Barbara Benoit.

Pages 180–181: *March 4, 1865.*
Lincoln, seated to the left of the speaking stand,
waits to deliver his second inaugural address.
This contemporary albumen print is the only known likeness
made from the lost original negative by Alexander Gardner.
Western Reserve Historical Society. (*Detail on page 181.*)

Head Quarters Armies of the United States,

City-Point,

Lieut Gen. Grant.   April 7. 11 AM. 1865

Gen. Sheridan says "If the thing is pressed I think that Lee will surrender." Let the *thing* be pressed.

A. LINCOLN

Lincoln's last order to General Grant

Fellow citizens: I am very greatly rejoiced to find that an occasion has occurred so pleasurable that the people cannot restrain themselves. [Cheers.] I suppose that arrangements are being made for some sort of a formal demonstration, this, or perhaps, to-morrow night. [Cries of 'We can't wait,' 'We want it now,' &c.] If there should be such a demonstration, I, of course, will be called upon to respond, and I shall have nothing to say if you dribble it all out of me before. [Laughter and applause.] I see you have a band of music with you. [Voices, 'We have two or three.'] I propose closing up this interview by the band performing a particular tune which I will name. Before this is done, however, I wish to mention one or two little circumstances connected with it. I have always thought 'Dixie' one of the best tunes I have ever heard. Our adversaries over the way attempted to appropriate it, but I insisted yesterday that we fairly captured it. [Applause.] I presented the question to the Attorney General, and he gave it as his legal opinion that it is our lawful prize. [Laughter and applause.] I now request the band to favor me with its performance.

Remarks to a crowd of delirious serenaders at the White House,
April 10, 1865; cited in the Washington *Daily National Intelligencer*

Lincoln at the age of fifty-six.
Gelatin silver print of a lost period print
of the multiple-image stereographic pose made by Alexander Gardner,
in Washington, D.C., between early February and mid-April 1865.
Mellon Collection.

The Second Inaugural Address
March 4, 1865

Fellow Countrymen:

At this second appearing to take the oath of the presidential office, there is less occasion for an extended address than there was at the first. Then a statement, somewhat in detail, of a course to be pursued, seemed fitting and proper. Now, at the expiration of four years, during which public declarations have been constantly called forth on every point and phase of the great contest which still absorbs the attention, and engrosses the energies of the nation, little that is new could be presented. The progress of our arms, upon which all else chiefly depends, is as well known to the public as to myself; and it is, I trust, reasonably satisfactory and encouraging to all. With high hope for the future, no prediction in regard to it is ventured.

On the occasion corresponding to this four years ago, all thoughts were anxiously directed to an impending civil-war. All dreaded it—all sought to avert it. While the inaugural address was being delivered from this place, devoted altogether to *saving* the Union without war, insurgent agents were in the city seeking to *destroy* it without war—seeking to dissolve the Union, and divide effects, by negotiation. Both parties deprecated war; but one of them would *make* war rather than let the nation survive; and the other would *accept* war rather than let it perish. And the war came.

One eighth of the whole population were colored slaves, not distributed generally over the Union, but localized in the Southern part of it. These slaves constituted a peculiar and powerful interest. All knew that this interest was, somehow, the cause of the war. To strengthen, perpetuate, and extend this interest was the object for which the insurgents would rend the Union, even by war; while the government claimed no right to do more than to restrict the territorial enlargement of it. Neither party expected for the war, the magnitude, or the duration, which it has already attained. Neither anticipated that the *cause* of the conflict might cease with, or even

before, the conflict itself should cease. Each looked for an easier triumph, and a result less fundamental and astounding. Both read the same Bible, and pray to the same God; and each invokes His aid against the other. It may seem strange that any men should dare to ask a just God's assistance in wringing their bread from the sweat of other men's faces; but let us judge not that we be not judged. The prayers of both could not be answered; that of neither has been answered fully. The Almighty has His own purposes. "Woe unto the world because of offences! for it must needs be that offences come; but woe to that man by whom the offence cometh!" If we shall suppose that American Slavery is one of those offences which, in the providence of God, must needs come, but which, having continued through His appointed time, He now wills to remove, and that He gives to both North and South, this terrible war, as the woe due to those by whom the offence came, shall we discern therein any departure from those divine attributes which the believers in a Living God always ascribe to Him?

Fondly do we hope—fervently do we pray—that this mighty scourge of war may speedily pass away. Yet, if God wills that it continue, until all the wealth piled by the bond-man's two hundred and fifty years of unrequited toil shall be sunk, and until every drop of blood drawn with the lash, shall be paid by another drawn with the sword, as was said three thousand years ago, so still it must be said "the judgments of the Lord, are true and righteous altogether."

With malice toward none; with charity for all; with firmness in the right, as God gives us to see the right, let us strive on to finish the work we are in; to bind up the nation's wounds; to care for him who shall have borne the battle, and for his widow, and his orphan— to do all which may achieve and cherish a just, and a lasting peace, among ourselves, and with all nations.

Traditionally known as the last photograph of Lincoln from life,
this contemporary albumen print is the only likeness
known to have been made from the broken, and soon discarded,
original negative made by Alexander Gardner, in Washington, D.C.,
between early February and mid-April 1865. Meserve Collection.

58

A Premonitory Dream

About ten days ago, I retired very late. I had been up waiting for important dispatches from the front. I could not have been long in bed when I fell into a slumber, for I was weary. I soon began to dream. There seemed to be a death-like stillness about me. Then I heard subdued sobs, as if a number of people were weeping. I thought I left my bed and wandered downstairs. There the silence was broken by the same pitiful sobbing, but the mourners were invisible. I went from room to room; no living person was in sight, but the same mournful sounds of distress met me as I passed along. It was light in all the rooms; every object was familiar to me; but where were all the people who were grieving as if their hearts would break? I was puzzled and alarmed. What could be the meaning of all this? Determined to find the cause of a state of things so mysterious and so shocking, I kept on until I arrived at the East Room, which I entered. There I met with a sickening surprise. Before me was a catafalque, on which rested a corpse wrapped in funeral vestments. Around it were stationed soldiers who were acting as guards; and there was a throng of people, some gazing mournfully upon the corpse, whose face was covered, others weeping pitifully. "Who is dead in the White House?" I demanded of one of the soldiers. "The President," was his answer; "he was killed by an assassin!" Then came a loud burst of grief from the crowd, which awoke me from my dream. I slept no more that night; and although it was only a dream, I have been strangely annoyed by it ever since.

Lincoln, in his last days,
to Ward Lamon and other dinner guests at the White House;
cited in Lamon, *Recollections of Abraham Lincoln*

Only surviving posthumous photograph of Lincoln.
Flanked by Admiral Charles Davis (left) and General Edward Townsend,
the President's body lies in state at City Hall, New York.
Contemporary albumen print from one frame of the lost original multiple-image
stereographic negative, made by Jeremiah Gurney, Jr., on April 24, 1865,
and destroyed shortly thereafter. Illinois State Historical Library.

Pages 8 and 162: The surviving oval-shaped albumen prints bearing the Brady imprint show more of the plate but normally contain less tone and reveal less detail in Lincoln's face than do the best surviving rectangular albumen prints, one of which is reproduced on page 162. While many of the latter are definitely originals, all of the former may be copies. A positive printed on film is reproduced on page 8 to illustrate the dilapidation of the original negative as it is today.

Pages 10 and 11, 78 and 79: On retiring in 1865, the photographer Alexander Hesler sold his gallery in Chicago to George B. Ayres, who acquired therewith the negatives of these two poses. Ayres sold the gallery in 1867 but kept the negatives, thereby sparing them from destruction in a fire at the gallery several weeks later or in the great Chicago fire of 1871. After distributing a few prints in the 1880s, Ayres expanded the practice and in the 1890s sold large numbers of the familiar albumen prints and platinum prints, which he normally signed on the reverse side. Most, but not all, of these were printed from glass copy negatives of various sizes, three of which survive in the collection of Dr. Maury Bromsen, of Boston, Massachusetts. Original prints of the profile pose also survive in Dr. Bromsen's collection and in that of the compiler. The original negatives were broken in the mail in 1933 and are now in the Smithsonian Institution. Film positives printed from these negatives for the purposes of this book reveal that their emulsion has darkened and that neither can give as fine a print today as it did formerly. Consequently, the reproductions on pages 10 and 11 are from original prints made in the 1930s. A pair of glass positive plates made around the turn of the century, probably at the behest of Ayres, from the original negatives are the finest surviving images of both poses; photographs of the two are reproduced on pages 78 and 79.

Above left: *Gelatin silver print of a lost retouched albumen print of a pose made by an unknown photographer, presumably in Washington, D.C., about 1864.* Mellon Collection.

Above right: *Reproduced from a positive printed on film from a defective period negative of a pose made by Anthony Berger at Mathew Brady's gallery, in Washington, D.C., April 20, 1864.* Ostendorf Collection.

Page 15: Two frames of the original multiple-image stereographic negative survive. One is at Brown University, the other in the Ostendorf Collection. Each is broken across the bottom, and the alignment of the broken edges indicates that the original glass negative suffered a single break through two of the lower stereo frames before they were separated. The unbroken negative frame owned by Harvey Leat, of Bethesda, Maryland, was not made by the collodion process and for this reason cannot be an original. It is a dry plate that probably dates from the 1880s or 1890s.

Page 19: Long treasured by the Lincoln family, this daguerreotype and the companion daguerreotype of Mrs. Lincoln were finally given to the Library of Congress in 1937 by Mary Lincoln Isham, a granddaughter of the President. A copy negative made of the exposed original immediately after it was cleaned at George Eastman House in 1949 gives the best reproducible image.

Page 21: The Lincoln authority Ida Tarbell wrote that George Schneider, the former editor of the *Staats-Zeitung*, a German-language, pro-Republican newspaper in Chicago in the 1850s, related to her in 1896 that this portrait originated as a daguerreotype made in Chicago at Schneider's request and in his presence by J. C. F. Polycarpus Von Schneidau. George Schneider wrote on a copy print that the sitting took place on August 9, 1854, but his memory appears to have failed him as to the precise date, for Lincoln was not in Chicago that day.

In their published works, the Lincoln authorities Frederick Meserve, Stefan Lorant, and Lloyd Ostendorf have dated the sitting in 1858, presumably because in some copy prints the masthead of the newspaper Lincoln is holding appears to be that of the Chicago *Press and Tribune*, a paper that gave Lincoln extensive favorable coverage that year during his race against Douglas. (Lorant and Ostendorf date the sitting July 11, when Lincoln is reported to have dined with Schneider and other Republican leaders in Chicago.) However, Ostendorf has subsequently proved that the masthead of the newspaper as it appears in the copy prints does not correspond in form to the actual masthead. Thus, where it appears in a copy print, the masthead has been painted into the picture and can have no bearing on the history of this pose. More important still, the Lincoln authority Bruce Duncan has determined that Von Schneidau, who is recognized by all authorities as the photographer, left the United States in July 1855 and did not return until 1859, when he was dying. This fact lends renewed force to George Schneider's claim that the sitting took place in 1854, and the earlier date, coupled with the fact that Von Schneidau was a known daguerreotypist, buttresses Schneider's claim that the portrait originated as a daguerreotype.

Duncan is now supported by Ostendorf in his belief that the sitting took place in late October 1854, when Schneider, Lincoln, and Von Schneidau were all in Chicago for several days. In any event, this portrait is Lincoln's second earliest known photographic pose. It is reproduced from a photograph of a lost period copy print that was once owned by George Schneider and was later acquired by the Lincoln collector Oliver Barrett.

A framed ambrotype copy showing only Lincoln's head and shoulders was owned in 1930 by William Brunyate, of Newark, New Jersey. Though efforts to locate this ambrotype have failed, photographs of it indicate that it retained more definition than does any known copy print on paper of the entire image; consequently, it may well have been made directly from the original likeness. Tarbell learned from Brunyate that he had obtained the ambrotype from a family that claimed to have acquired it in Mattoon, Illinois, during Lincoln's lifetime.

Page 22: A last-minute attempt by the photographer and by Lincoln himself to comb his "wild republican hair" with their fingers resulted in the famous "tousled hair photograph"—a portrait that poignantly recalls Lincoln's quip that his hair had "a way of getting up as far as possible in the world." The negative is thought to have been destroyed either in 1867 or in 1871 when fires gutted the former Hesler gallery; however, a number of original albumen prints, at least two of which are signed, have survived. The only known albumen original bearing the imprint of Hesler's gallery is in the collection of the Illinois State Historical Library. In the 1880s and 1890s, George B. Ayres, who had acquired the Hesler gallery in 1865 and had managed it for two years, distributed copy prints of this pose.

Page 24: In 1908, a Civil War veteran named William Hilyard, of Superior, Nebraska, sent to the Lincoln authority Frederick Meserve a photograph of an ambrotype of Lincoln then in his possession. Hilyard wrote that the ambrotype had belonged to his father, Thomas Hilyard, a deputy sheriff in Vermilion County, Illinois, who appears to have claimed that he and his friend Lincoln once sat for the photographer Amon J. T. Joslin at his gallery in Danville, Illinois, and that they then exchanged photographic likenesses. The image is reproduced here from a copy ambrotype that retains more tone and definition than do the surviving photographs of the Hilyard ambrotype. The compiler regards it as likely that the lost Hilyard ambrotype was also a copy—that the photographer may have made several copy ambrotypes but that he probably kept the original likeness for the purposes of reproduction. All attempts to date the sitting depend on Hilyard's assertion that it took place in Danville. Meserve gives the date as November 1859, when Lincoln visited the town. Clint Tilton, the late president of the Illinois State Historical Society, claimed to have determined that the correct date was late April or early May 1858, when Lincoln was attending sessions of the Vermilion County circuit court in and around Danville. The Lincoln authority Lloyd Ostendorf gives as the most likely date May 1857, at the end of Lincoln's attendance at the same court sessions a year earlier. The sitting has been dated as early as 1853, simply because Lincoln was in Danville that year. The Hilyard ambrotype was last reported in the possession of J. P. Hilyard, who owned it in 1954.

Page 26: In his book *Life on the Circuit with Lincoln*, H. C. Whitney, Lincoln's friend and fellow lawyer, leaves an eyewitness account of this sitting. The pose survives today thanks mainly to W. H. Somers, who in 1885 had a copy negative, now lost, made from a retouched print of the original ambrotype and permitted the photographer A. R. Campbell, of Beatrice, Nebraska, to print mounted copies, one of which is reproduced. The large thumb mark that is visible on every surviving copy print of this pose was made either on the wet collodion of the ambrotype itself or on the copy negative.

Page 29: The original ambrotype was willed by the photographer's widow to the University of Nebraska in 1947. An ambrotype copy possessing far less definition than the original was for many years exhibited at the Lincoln tomb, in Springfield, Illinois. The compiler's efforts to locate it have proven fruitless, but a few copy prints of it survive.

Page 31: Possibly the most revealing portrait of the beardless Lincoln, this riveting ambrotype was for many years owned by James K. Magie, of Macomb, Illinois. Magie claimed he had received the likeness from Lincoln, after accompanying him to T. P. Pearson's gallery, in Macomb, on August 26, 1858. In 1866, W. J. Franklin, also of Macomb, made from the original ambrotype a copy negative, which is now lost. The two prints known to have been made from this negative are also lost, but photographs of them were obtained, copied, and widely distributed by the Lincoln authority Frederick Meserve. Richard Watson Gilder, editor of the *Century*, acquired the ambrotype from Magie in 1886 or 1887 and had an exceptionally fine copy negative made of it. A print from this lost negative is reproduced. The ambrotype is thought to have been destroyed in 1888 when a fire swept the Century building and gutted Gilder's office. A small number of cartes-de-visite of this pose were printed by the S. P. Tresize gallery, in Springfield, Illinois. At least two ambrotype copies of the original have survived: one is in the Ostendorf Collection; the other is in the collection of Carl Haverlin, of Northridge, California.

Page 32: The original ambrotype was owned in the 1890s by A. Montgomery, of Columbus, Ohio. Montgomery claimed that the likeness had been given to him by Sylvester Strong, of Atlanta, Illinois, who told him he had received it from Lincoln for having acted as the latter's host during one of his visits to Atlanta. The ambrotype is thought to date from shortly before or shortly after Lincoln's visit to Atlanta on July 17, 1858.

Page 33: Almost nothing is known about this pose. A photograph of what appears, judging from the frame, to have been an ambrotype was sent to the Lincoln authority Frederick Meserve by the late A. L. Maresh, of Cleveland, Ohio. Meserve's minimum-second-generation copy prints, one of which is reproduced, may well be the only surviving images.

Page 34: This pose became one of Lincoln's best-known beardless portraits, largely because he himself was so fond of it. Mounted signed prints, at least a dozen of which survive, and one of which is reproduced, were among his favorite gifts to friends and relatives. The known ambrotypes of this pose are all copies, first, because they lack the definition of the best surviving albumen prints, and second, because they encompass less of the total image than do some of the prints. Though the identity of the photographer and the place of the sitting remain subjects of controversy, Roderick M. Cole, of Peoria, Illinois, is still the only photographer known to have claimed in writing that he made this portrait. In a letter dated July 3, 1905, to Judge McCulloch, a founder of the Illinois State Historical Library, Cole identified this pose as his work, described the sitting with Lincoln in some detail, dated it as having occurred during the Lincoln-Douglas campaign, and stated that the portrait had originated as a daguerreotype. This last point the compiler has difficulty accepting. If the original portrait was a daguerreotype, then all the surviving albumen prints are copies. However, the extraordinary clarity of some of these paper prints convinces the compiler that they could not be copies and that therefore this portrait must have originated as a collodion negative made for printing. Finally, the discovery of so many signed prints and ambrotype copies of this pose in the vicinity of Springfield, Illinois, has led the Lincoln authority Lloyd Ostendorf to regard Cole's claim with increasing doubt and to conjecture that perhaps this portrait was made by one of Lincoln's home-town photographers.

Page 37: The Lincoln authorities Frederick Meserve, Stefan Lorant, and Lloyd Ostendorf refer to this portrait as a ferrotype mainly, the compiler suspects, because the print on japanned iron, now owned by the National Park Service, in Washington, D.C., has long been the only well-known early image of the pose. However, this ferrotype, once owned by Osborn H. Oldroyd, former custodian of the Lincoln home in Springfield, Illinois, is a minimum-fourth-generation copy. Indeed, the succeeding generations of copies, all clearly distinguishable in the surviving likenesses, make this one of the most curious, most interesting pictures of Lincoln. Whether the original was a ferrotype cannot be determined. Minimum-third-generation copy prints on paper were made by the Lincoln authority Truman Bartlett from a now lost copy negative. One of these is reproduced.

Pages 39 and 193: After the photographer's death, his son, John N. Thomson, had the fading original ambrotype photographed in Monmouth, Illinois, by John Nicol, in 1883. A single copy print bearing the imprint of Nicol's gallery was sent to Lincoln's son Robert, from whom it eventually passed to Robert Lincoln Beckwith, the great-grandson and last surviving descendant of the President. Recently acquired from Beckwith by James T. Hickey, of the Illinois State Historical Library, the faded Nicol print (see page 193, upper right) may be the only surviving unretouched image of this pose. In 1896, Margaret Taggart Thomson, the photographer's widow, permitted Colonel Clark Carr to have the original ambrotype photographed at the Harrison gallery, in Galesburg, Illinois, for the first publication of this pose, by Ida Tarbell, in *McClure's* magazine. Thereafter, for thirty years, the gallery sold under its imprint the familiar retouched copy prints of this pose (see page 39). Prior to 1935, when he died, John N. Thomson claimed that the original ambrotype was last owned by one of his relatives in San Francisco, but that by then it had faded to complete indistinctness.

Pages 40 and 42: In September 1858, midway through the Lincoln-Douglas debates, Mrs. Harriet Chapman, of Charleston, Illinois, the granddaughter of Lincoln's stepmother, asked Lincoln to send her his photograph. In due course, a likeness of this pose arrived by mail from Springfield.

Appearing on page 40 is a quarter-plate daguerreotype copy, formerly in the collection of A. Conger Goodyear and previously owned by the Lincoln authority and collector William Lambert, of a lost oval-shaped likeness that reveals more detail in Lincoln's face than does any known print on paper. This lost likeness, which was probably the original image, may well have been a full-plate daguerreotype. Or it may have been an ambrotype. However, it reveals too much detail of skin surface in Lincoln's face to have been an 1858 print on paper. Indeed, the compiler is convinced that all the known prints on paper of this pose, including the signed print, are photographs of a lost image on either glass or copper.

Goodyear wrote that he received with the daguerreotype a letter in which R. N. Chapman referred to the photographic likeness that his mother, Harriet Chapman, had received from Lincoln. Whether in this letter, which appears to be lost, Chapman was referring to the surviving daguerreotype copy or merely to this pose of Lincoln or to another likeness of this pose is not known. However, the Lincoln authority Frederick Meserve wrote that Lambert, who owned the daguerreotype copy for many years before Goodyear acquired it, "was unable to give the compiler [Meserve] its history . . ."

A number of contemporary albumen copy prints of this pose survive, and one of these, possibly the only remaining of two prints that Lincoln is known to have signed, is reproduced on page 42. Originally presented by Lincoln to Arnold Robinson, the court crier in Springfield, this print was subsequently owned by Robinson's widow, who sold it to the Illinois State Historical Library. It was then acquired by the Lincoln authority and collector Oliver Barrett, whose estate auctioned the picture in 1952. Subsequently owned by the manuscript dealer King

---

*Upper left: Rare unretouched contemporary albumen print
from the lost original negative believed to have been made by William Shaw,
probably in Chicago or Springfield, during the spring
or summer of 1860. Ostendorf Collection.*

*Upper right: Made from a lost copy negative,
this faded albumen print is the only known unretouched likeness
of the lost original ambrotype made by William Judkins Thomson, in Monmouth,
Illinois, October 11, 1858. Courtesy of James T. Hickey.*

*Lower left: Solio print of a lost original ambrotype
made by Preston Butler, in Springfield, Illinois, August 13, 1860, for use
by the miniature portraitist John Henry Brown. Mellon Collection.*

*Lower right: Gelatin silver print
of a heavily retouched contemporary albumen print from a lost negative
made by an unknown photographer, in Springfield, Illinois,
during May or June 1860. Mellon Collection.*

V. Hostick, of Springfield, Illinois, it was again purchased at auction in 1977, this time by Dr. Benjamin Weisinger, who gave it to the present owner.

Page 45: After Colonel Gilmer's death in the Civil War, the original ambrotype was owned for many years by his daughter Elizabeth. It eventually appeared in the collection of C. F. Gunther, of Chicago, and was later acquired by the noted collector of Lincolniana, Oliver Barrett. In 1952, the ambrotype was auctioned with the rest of Barrett's collection by the Parke-Bernet Galleries, in New York City. The compiler has not been able to determine the identity of the buyer or the present whereabouts of the ambrotype. A surviving ambrotype copy lacking both the tone and the definition of the Gilmer original was made for Charles Lame, of Pittsfield, Illinois, and was owned for many years by his grandson the Rev. Henry Morton, of Wichita Falls, Texas. An apparent tintype copy, framed and under glass, survives in the Washington State Historical Society, at Tacoma. Its donor, Frank C. Ross, was a grandson of Colonel William Ross, who had been one of Lincoln's hosts in Pittsfield during the Senate race of 1858.

A number of copy prints of this pose remain, but only the one reproduced here shows the magnificent original in a near facsimile of its full detail. The later copy prints reveal a wash of scratches across Lincoln's face, indicating that the original ambrotype, wherever it may be, has been severely damaged.

Page 49: One authority attributes this pose to William Seavy, of Canton, Illinois, on the tenuous ground that there is a similarity between Lincoln's appearance here and his appearance in the known Seavy portrait (see page 53). Equally dubious is a claim by the Lincoln authority Herbert Wells Fay, former custodian of the Lincoln tomb, that Frederick Gutekunst, of Philadelphia, was the photographer.

Page 51: The original negative is lost, and not a single original print or unretouched print is known to survive. Cartes-de-visite and a few larger prints, all made from lost copy negatives of lost retouched original prints, are the only known period likenesses of this famous pose.

Page 53: The earliest known owner of this print was N. S. Wright, of Springfield, Illinois. The negative appears to have been destroyed by fire, along with the photographer's gallery, in Canton, Illinois.

Page 54: The ambrotype is published here from the original for the first time. Joseph H. Barrett writes that it was made at his request and in his presence at a photographic gallery in Springfield, Illinois. He dates the sitting May 24, 1860, four days after the two companion poses (see pages 64 and 75) are known to have been made. The Lincoln authority Lloyd Ostendorf accepts that there were two sittings, primarily because Lincoln's bow tie is arranged differently in this pose. The compiler also finds evidence of two sittings in the fact that Marcus L. Ward, at whose request the May 20 sitting was arranged, and Barrett *both* claim to have prevailed upon Lincoln to sit for them in a local gallery, without either of them mentioning the other. Nevertheless, a strong argument can be made in favor of the theory that all three poses originated at the May 20 sitting. The condition of Lincoln's suit, vest, hair, and spectacles chain is virtually identical in the three poses. In all three, his suit and vest are immaculately cleaned and pressed. Would they still have looked that way four days later? Is it likely that Lincoln had them cleaned and pressed again in the three intervening days? Lincoln could easily have straightened his bow tie, with a mere flick of the fingers, during the sitting. Looking back on the event, Barrett could have erred by four days in dating the sitting. And, in their recollections, perhaps neither Barrett nor Ward wanted to share the credit for having persuaded Lincoln to sit for any of these poses.

Barrett appears to have given the ambrotype to his publisher, Frank Baldwin, of Cincinnati, Ohio. Baldwin left it to his nephew, Henry Ward, who gave Herbert Wells Fay, former custodian of the Lincoln tomb, permission to make copies of the original; hence the familiar prints that Fay signed and distributed. Ward's daughter Charlotte gave the ambrotype to the Nebraska State Historical Society in 1955.

Page 57: This glass positive, or lantern slide, and an accompanying nineteenth-century paper print were given to the Decatur (Illinois) Public Library in 1947 by the photographer's daughter, Grace Barnwell.

Page 58: In 1925, Gilbert Ross, of Lake Geneva, Wisconsin, sent to the Lincoln authority Frederick Meserve what is probably the only surviving original print of this pose. He claimed to have obtained it from his late neighbor, William Bane, in whose possession he had occasionally seen the photograph since about 1891. According to Ross, Bane claimed to have received the print from Lincoln in 1860, when he (Bane) was a livestock dealer resident in Charleston, Illinois. Relying, presumably, on what Bane had told him, Ross wrote in 1931 that "This photo is believed to be the approval print from a negative made in 1860 for political purposes, which negative was later sent to St. Paul, and broken in transit." Ross then suggests, "It is a silver print on albumen paper, presumably made in Chicago, and the mount has been somewhat inaccurately trimmed to the edge of the print, as tho to go in the same small package with the negative for shipment to Springfield, Ill."

All attempts to date the sitting precisely (within the first ten months of 1860) have depended on Ross's belief that it took place in Chicago. If, however, he believed this mainly because his print was "a silver print on albumen paper" (which the compiler feels is implied), he was not necessarily correct. Ross's original, which the compiler located in 1977, thirty-six years after Ross's death, is an ordinary gold-toned albumen print, which could just as easily have been made in Springfield or in numerous other places where Lincoln sojourned during the first ten months of 1860, when he was still beardless.

Page 59: The original negative of this pose is lost and no original print is known to survive. The only known nineteenth-century likeness is a mounted copy print that was obtained by the Lincoln authority Ida Tarbell from the heirs of the artist John Henry Brown. Tarbell left the print to Allegheny College.

Page 61: This pose may have been made for the sculptor Henry Kirke Brown, among whose effects the print reproduced here was found in 1931.

Upper left and right, lower right: *Cartes-de-visite*
printed from lost contemporary negatives, possibly originals, of the
views of three multiple-image stereographic poses made
by Alexander Gardner at Mathew Brady's gallery,
in Washington, D.C., about February 24, 1861.
Upper left: Brown University. Upper right: courtesy of David O'Reilly.
Lower right: courtesy of George Rinhart.

Lower left: *Gelatin silver print from a retouched period negative of*
a pose made by Christopher S. German, in Springfield, Illinois, January 13, 1861,
for use by the sculptor Thomas Jones. Ostendorf Collection.

Page 62: Lincoln sent the negative of this pose to M. C. Tuttle, of St. Paul, Minnesota, so that the latter could print campaign likenesses from it for the presidential race of 1860. According to one account, the negative was sent as the replacement for a negative that had been broken in the mail and that is believed to have been the negative of the pose that appears on page 58.

Page 64: This ambrotype is published here from the original for the first time. According to Marcus L. Ward, later governor of New Jersey, the likeness was made at his request and in his presence at a photographic gallery in Springfield on May 20, 1860. Not a single contemporary albumen print of this pose is known to have existed. The ambrotype was given by Ward's descendants to the Newark Public Library.

Pages 66 and 193: A somewhat indistinct mounted print, believed to be the only unretouched albumen original, survives in the Ostendorf Collection (see page 193, upper left). It bears the imprint of William Shaw, whose gallery was in Chicago but who may have photographed Lincoln in Springfield, Illinois. Two contemporary albumen prints, in which the backgrounds have been painted out, also survive; and while both may be copies of lost retouched originals, one of the two is reproduced here (see page 66) on account of its superior photographic qualities.

Page 68: This is the least known of the four poses made by Hesler in 1860 (see also pages 77, 78, and 79). The original negative is believed to have been destroyed in 1867 or 1871, when fires swept the photographer's gallery in Chicago.

Page 71: In 1923, when the photographer Joseph Hill was ninety years old, he wrote on the mat of one of his own copy prints of this pose that "this photo is made from an old print, the original negative of which was made by the undersigned a few days after his [Lincoln's] first nomination for the presidency, in Springfield, Illinois, in 1860, at his home." This suggests that the sitting occurred in late May or early June 1860. Discarded in a woodshed, the one original albumen print, which is now lost, escaped destruction when a fire gutted Hill's gallery in Springfield. The best surviving images are copy prints made by the photographer himself in old age. One of these is reproduced.

Page 73: In August 1860, Judge John Read, a Republican leader in Philadelphia who was dissatisfied with the current likenesses of Lincoln, sent the miniature portraitist John Henry Brown, of Philadelphia, to paint the Republican presidential candidate for a campaign engraving, which was later made by Samuel Sartain. In Springfield, Illinois, Brown engaged the photographer Preston Butler to make some ambrotypes of Lincoln, who presumably could not spare the time for extensive sittings. Of the half dozen ambrotypes which Butler made, all except this one appear to be lost, though the image of a second one is preserved in copy photographs (see page 193, lower left). Of Brown's painting, which was influenced by the surviving ambrotype, Lincoln wrote to Judge Read, "The miniature likeness of myself, taken by your friend, J. Henry Brown, is an excellent one, so far as I can judge. To my unpracticed eye, it is without fault." The ambrotype was acquired from the painter's son, W. P. Brown, by the Lincoln collector William Lambert. Later owned by A. Conger Goodyear, it was bequeathed with his collection to the Library of Congress in 1965.

Page 75: The existence of exceptionally clear albumen prints, signed and unsigned, of this pose indicates that the photographer retained the negative for the purposes of reproduction, though he ambrotyped the negatives of the two companion poses (see also pages 54 and 64), at least one of which was made at the same sitting as this pose.

Without citing any supporting evidence, the Lincoln authority Frederick Meserve attributes all three poses to William Church, of Springfield, Illinois. However, the Lincoln authority Lloyd Ostendorf counters that Church was not yet listed as a photographer in the 1860–1861 Springfield City Directory and that he is not known to have engaged in the profession there until 1866. Ostendorf suggests that William Marsh, who was listed as an ambrotypist in the 1860–1861 directory, may have been the photographer, but the only evidence he offers in support of this hunch is the similarity of the names, which he feels may have led Meserve into error. Ostendorf has determined that a law student named William Church was working in Lincoln's office in 1860; however, both Ostendorf and the compiler deem it highly unlikely that any of the three poses was the work of an amateur, because at least two are known, from eyewitness accounts, to have been made in photographic galleries and all three were posed as though by a professional.

The compiler believes that the three poses are the work of the Springfield photographer Preston Butler. On May 24, 1860, four days after this pose and at least one of the two companion poses were made, Butler advertised in the *Illinois State Journal* as follows: "P. Butler of this city has a number of photograph likenesses of Hon. Abraham Lincoln. He will sell them for one dollar each. . . ." Furthermore, Butler, who is believed to have photographed Lincoln once before (see page 32), made four poses of the presidential candidate on May 26, though none

Top: *Lincoln conferring with General McClellan.*
Reproduced from a positive printed on film from one frame
of the original multiple-image stereographic negative made for
Mathew Brady by Alexander Gardner, at Antietam, Maryland,
October 3, 1862. Library of Congress.

Lower left: *Lincoln seated by the table*
at which he signed the Emancipation Proclamation. Contemporary albumen print
from the lost original negative made at the White House
by Anthony Berger of Mathew Brady's gallery, April 26, 1864,
for use by the portrait painter Francis Carpenter.
Courtesy of Laurence Carpenter Ives.

Lower right: *Lincoln standing beside the table*
at which he signed the Emancipation Proclamation. Gelatin silver print
of a lost period print from the lost original negative
made at the White House by Anthony Berger of Mathew Brady's gallery,
April 26, 1864, for use by the portrait painter
Francis Carpenter. Mellon Collection.

of these is known to survive. Again, on June 7, the *Illinois State Journal* reported: "P. Butler has executed a miniature photograph of Mr. Lincoln, suitable for badges . . . price 10 cents each, or $6 per thousand. His larger photographs are the best we have seen, and are going off quick at one dollar each."

The Lincoln authority Ida Tarbell states that a print of this particular pose was owned by the artist John Henry Brown, for whom Butler is known to have made several ambrotypes of Lincoln in August 1860, ten weeks after the May sittings, and who may well have obtained the print from Butler along with the ambrotypes. Meserve states that this pose as well as the two companion poses were made expressly for Brown's use; however, the testimony of Marcus L. Ward and Joseph H. Barrett refutes this.

Lincoln signed at least two prints of this pose, one of which he sent to Benjamin Prescott, later governor of New Hampshire, and which is now in the New Hampshire Historical Society. The other is lost but survives in the form of a copy photograph in the Ostendorf Collection.

Page 77: The negative of this pose is believed to have been destroyed in 1867 or 1871, when fires gutted the photographer's gallery in Chicago. At least two signed prints are known to have existed, one of which survives in the collection of James T. Hickey, of Springfield, Illinois. However, the lost print, which is reproduced here from a copy photograph, reveals Lincoln's face in greater detail than does any other surviving image of this pose.

Page 80: Lincoln's friend and fellow lawyer H. C. Whitney is said to have owned the only print made from the lost original negative. Around 1890, Herbert Wells Fay, then custodian of the Lincoln tomb, obtained from the Chicago photographer C. D. Mosher a carte-de-visite copy of what appears to have been a retouched original print. Fay and the Lincoln authority Frederick Meserve later distributed a number of copy prints of the Fay carte, and it is from these that the pose is known today. The carte itself may have survived in Fay's now inaccessible collection, which is currently owned by the heirs of the late Paul Nehring, of DeKalb, Illinois.

Pages 81 and 195: Contemporary albumen prints, signed as well as unsigned, exist of the pose on page 81 and of an almost identical companion pose shown on page 195, lower left, both of which were made for use by the sculptor Thomas Jones, who accompanied Lincoln to the sitting. A retouched contemporary negative, possibly the original but now broken, of the companion pose is known to survive in the collection of the late Lincoln authority Herbert Wells Fay, custodian of the Lincoln tomb. Inaccessible at present, his collection is currently owned by the heirs of the late Paul Nehring, of DeKalb, Illinois. Fay distributed numerous prints from the retouched negative, which is marred by artwork around the eyes,

also on the profile of Lincoln's left cheek and on the facial skin. An early print from Fay's negative served as the model from which the likeness on the original greenback ten-dollar bill was engraved.

Page 82: A collodion copy negative made from a contemporary albumen print of this pose survives in the Meserve Collection.

Page 85: Two contemporary albumen prints of this pose are known to survive: the cabinet-sized print reproduced here, which may be the only original, and the one known carte-de-visite (at Brown University), which the Lincoln authority Frederick Meserve distributed in copy form, and which, on account of its comparative lack of definition, was almost certainly made from a lost copy negative.

Page 86: Among the best-preserved original negatives of Lincoln are the two surviving frames of this stereographic pose. Both are in the Meserve Collection. The frames of an almost identical companion pose (see page 195, lower right) are lost.

Page 89: In all probability, not a single unretouched image of this pose exists. The known original salt prints have undergone varying amounts of artwork, while the cartes-de-visite and larger albumen prints are copies of lost retouched originals.

That the known period prints of this pose bear the imprints of so many different photographers and photographic galleries merely attests to the rampant plagiarism of the photographic profession in Lincoln's time. The identity of the photographer is still not known.

The discovery of a carte-de-visite print of this pose on a ticket to an 1861 Independence Day fireworks display, and the fact that Lincoln's hair is shorter here than it was in the poses made by Gardner on or about February 21 of that year, enabled Ostendorf to date this sitting as no earlier than late February and no later than the end of June 1861. Furthermore, since Lincoln did not leave the capital during the first four months of the war, the sitting must have taken place in Washington, D.C.

The J. B. Speed Art Museum's signed original salt print, which Lincoln inscribed to Mrs. Lucy G. Speed on October 3, 1861 and which bears the longest known inscription of any Lincoln photograph, has now faded almost to indistinctness, though prints from the museum's copy negative, made in 1953, give a convincing impression of the vanishing image. A similar signed print of this pose was inscribed and sent in an identical frame to Mrs. Speed's daughter-in-law Fanny; it is reproduced here.

Neither the original negative nor any period copy negative of this pose is known to survive.

A similar, but definitely distinct, pose made at the same sitting survives in

Upper left: *Carte-de-visite printed from a lost contemporary negative of one view of a multiple-image stereographic pose made by Anthony Berger at Mathew Brady's gallery, in Washington, D.C., February 9, 1864.* Ostendorf Collection.

Upper right: *Carte-de-visite printed from a contemporary negative of one view of a multiple-image stereographic pose made by Mathew Brady, in Washington, D.C., January 8, 1864.* Mellon Collection.

Lower left: *Carte-de-visite printed from one frame of the lost original multiple-image stereographic negative made by Alexander Gardner, in Washington, D.C., August 9, 1863.* Ostendorf Collection.

Lower right: *Lincoln and his son Tad. Gelatin silver print of a carte-de-visite that is the only known unvignetted likeness of the pose (see page 152) made by Anthony Berger at Mathew Brady's gallery, in Washington, D.C., February 9, 1864.* Ostendorf Collection.

the form of a single carte-de-visite in the Ostendorf Collection; it is published here for the first time on pages 92 and 93.

Page 95: The Lincoln authority Stefan Lorant states that this image is a retouched print of the well-known pose reproduced on page 89. However, after superimposing positives on film of these two images and after subjecting them to every other known test for distinctness, the compiler is forced to conclude that the two definitely originated from significantly different negatives and that they are therefore distinct poses. The carte-de-visite reproduced here, which was first identified as a new Lincoln pose by Lloyd Ostendorf in 1956, bears the imprint of the Bierstadt brothers, and Edward Bierstadt's presence in the vicinity of Washington, D.C., during the summer of 1861 raises the possibility that he may have been the photographer.

Pages 97; 101; 105; 120; 123; 147; 160; 195, upper left and upper right; and 199, lower left: Cartes-de-visite are the only period likenesses known to have been printed from the lost contemporary negatives of these multiple-image stereographic poses.

Page 103: Measuring 18⅛ by 20⅜ inches, the surviving glass plate of this pose is the largest original collodion negative known to have been made of Lincoln. Three stereographic poses made with a multiple-lens camera (see pages 97, 101, and 105) and one pose made with a single-lens camera (see page 99) appear to have originated at the same sitting.

Pages 110–111: This is the only photograph of Lincoln that the photographer Alexander Gardner included in *Gardner's Photographic Sketchbook of the War*.

Page 123: Lieutenant John L. Cunningham recalled in his diary that on April 17, 1863, he and two other officers watched Lincoln posing for a full-length photograph by Thomas Le Mere at Mathew Brady's gallery, in Washington, D.C. The Lincoln authority Lloyd Ostendorf believes that the pose reproduced here was probably the one referred to by Cunningham, simply because the dates of the sittings at which all of the other known full-length poses of the bearded Lincoln were made have been ascertained, and none of these sittings took place on April 17, 1863. However, the compiler remains dubious. This pose bears a strong resemblance to the five poses that were made by an unknown photographer at Mathew Brady's gallery, in Washington, D.C., about 1862 (see pages 97, 99, 101, 103, 105). Points of resemblance include the condition of Lincoln's hair, beard, and clothing, his watch chain, and the chair behind him.

Page 124: The print reproduced here originally belonged to Lincoln's secretary, John Hay, and is currently owned by his grandson, also John Hay. A probable original and the only known likeness of this pose, the print caused a sensation when in 1969 it was first published by the Lincoln authority Lloyd Ostendorf in the summer issue of the *Lincoln Herald* and shortly thereafter, for nationwide circulation, by the Lincoln authority Stefan Lorant in *Look* magazine.

Page 127: The stereo angles of the surviving prints of this pose prove conclusively that the original stereographic negative contained at least six images and that the plate was therefore made with a camera that had at least two horizontal tiers of lenses, one tier above the other, with at least three lenses in each tier. No other minimum-six-lens stereographic pose of Lincoln is known to have been made, though some of the presumed two-lens, three-lens, and four-lens stereographs, especially the three that Gardner made on the same day as this one, may have originated as six-lens poses.

The known period prints of this pose, which include one carte-de-visite owned by Harold Holzer, of New York City, an albumen print of carte-de-visite size, reproduced here, and several prints which survive only as copies, all lack definition, if not also tone. The compiler is therefore convinced that the original negative plate that included the frames from which the surviving images originate must have been defective.

Page 128: The Lincoln National Life Foundation has an albumen print of *imperial* size that bears the Gardner imprint and that may be the only remaining contemporary original. However, the familiar prints made by the photographer M. P. Rice, around 1900, from the lost original negative are the best surviving images.

Page 138: Misplaced and lost for decades in the National Archives, the original negative of this view of Lincoln attending the ceremony at which he delivered the Gettysburg Address was finally rediscovered by the archivist Josephine Cobb in 1953.

Pages 143 and 145: Among the known prints of this pose, the one that shows Lincoln in the fullest detail is a print in which the two secretaries have, unfortunately, been cropped out.

Page 147: Originally acquired by a Civil War drummer boy named Pearson Snyder Clime, the two surviving frames of the original stereographic negative remained in the Clime family until 1956, when they were purchased, in damaged condition, by the Lincoln authority Lloyd Ostendorf. The photographer, Lewis E. Walker, worked in the office of the Supervising Architect of the Treasury. The image is reproduced from a carte-de-visite—one of the half dozen printed by Walker in May 1865 at the request of John Meigs for the New York artist J. W. Dodge, who was painting Lincoln posthumously.

Pages 148 and 149: Lincoln authorities have long been baffled as to who made the two familiar multiple-image stereographs known as the "crew-cut" poses. The compiler has determined that both were made by Lewis E. Walker, a photographer working in the office of the Supervising Architect of the Treasury. On the back of a carte-de-visite of one of the poses there appears in the hand of Walker's friend John Meigs, "Negative by Walker—Phot'rep U.S. Treas'y Dept. Wash. D.C." The inscription is dated June 12, 1865. The New York photographic firm of E. & H. T. Anthony printed a few stereographic cards and numerous cartes-de-visite of the two poses, but the identity of the photographer remained a matter of speculation until 1977.

Page 151: The two known contemporary albumen prints made from the lost original negative cannot be located. The pose may therefore survive only in the form of photographs of these lost prints. Copy negatives survive in the Library of Congress, the National Archives, and the Meserve Collection.

Pages 152 and 199: Lincoln signed several prints of this pose, at least two of them with the unusual autograph "A. Lincoln & Son." The only known unretouched print showing the full image was a carte-de-visite that belonged to the late F. Ray Risdon (see page 199, lower right). Since the Risdon carte lacks definition, the pose is also reproduced from a vignetted original print (see page 152). The Lincoln authority Lloyd Ostendorf claims to have detected slight traces of a stereographic relationship between some of the surviving prints. This raises the possibility that the pose may have originated as a multiple-image stereograph.

Pages 154 and 190: All of the surviving period prints of the pose on page 154 and its companion pose, on page 190, left, are vignetted. All but a few are retouched cartes-de-visite printed by the firm of Wenderoth and Taylor of Philadelphia after Lincoln's assassination. No original negative or contemporary copy negative of either pose is known to survive.

Pages 158, 159, and 161: Three or more frames of contemporary negatives of each of these multiple-image stereographic poses survive, but authorities differ as to which are originals and which are merely very fine copies.

Page 166: The portrait painter Francis Carpenter appears to have cut Lincoln's head out of the only known original print of this pose. The sketchbook into which he pasted the cut-out head is owned by his great-grandson, Laurence Carpenter Ives.

Pages 169 and 190: The original negative of the pose on page 169 and a defective period negative of a companion pose (see page 190, right) belonged to the portrait painter Francis Carpenter. Both plates remained in the possession of his family until they were purchased by the Lincoln authority Lloyd Ostendorf in 1956. The broken triangular negative was first published in 1947 by the Lincoln authority Stefan Lorant in the *Saturday Evening Post* by permission of the artist's grandson, Emerson Carpenter Ives.

Pages 172 and 199: Two frames from the original stereographic negative of the pose on page 172 and one frame from the original stereographic negative of a companion pose (see page 199, upper left) survive in the Meserve Collection.

Pages 174, 175, 177, 185, 187: The so-called "Last Photographs of Lincoln": The correct date of this famous sitting has become the central question in a mounting controversy. It was Frederick Meserve who gave birth to the durable tradition that these five portraits were the last photographic likenesses made of the living President. After receiving, in 1913, the only known print of the most famous of these poses from his friend and fellow Lincoln authority Truman Bartlett, Meserve wrote that Bartlett had related to him how he had acquired this print from the photographer Alexander Gardner in 1874 and that Gardner had told him that the sitting had taken place about April 10, 1865, five days before the President's death. There also exists a carte-de-visite of one of the five Gardner poses on the back of which is written in the hand of an early owner, "The last photograph of President Lincoln—Taken in Washington . . . five days before his assassination. Presented by Major Pool, who met the President coming out of the gallery immediately after the picture was taken."

However, other evidence suggests that the sitting may have taken place on February 5, 1865, and that therefore the five famous Gardner poses may not be the last photographs of the living President after all. The portrait painter Matthew Wilson left a diary in which he mentions having "at 2 o'clock met Mr. Lincoln at Gardner's" on February 5, 1865. In his entry of the previous day, Wilson states that he "Went to Gardner's rooms in the morning." This may well have been to arrange a sitting for Lincoln. Subsequently, between February 7 and 20, Wilson painted a portrait of the President that bears a striking resemblance to one of the Gardner photographs. Furthermore, the Lincoln authority Lloyd Ostendorf has a print of one of the poses made by Henry F. Warren on March 6 that bears the photographer's imprint and is captioned "The Last Photograph of President Lincoln." He also argues that the surviving cartes-de-visite of the Gardner poses, which have neither black mourning borders nor captions indicating the President's demise, must have been printed while he was yet living. Ostendorf maintains that if the sitting had taken place as late as April 10, Lincoln's first full day in Washington after returning from Richmond, there would hardly have been time to print, mount, and caption several issues of cartes-de-visite in the four days of life that the President had left. After weighing all the known evidence, the compiler has decided that the date of this sitting cannot yet be determined with certainty.

Pages 174, 175, and 185: From the lost contemporary negatives of these poses, which included copy plates as well as the originals, cartes-de-visite and larger prints in various sizes were made. The surviving likenesses include vignetted and full-plate prints, some of which are retouched, others not.

Page 187: Frederick Meserve recorded the history of this famous portrait on the back of the only known original, a contemporary albumen print that is reproduced. He wrote that his fellow Lincoln authority Truman Bartlett had given him the print in 1913; that Bartlett claimed to have acquired it from the photographer Alexander Gardner in 1874; that, according to Bartlett, Gardner had claimed that this pose was the last taken by him, on or around April 10, 1865, at a sitting that had been the living President's last appearance before the camera, and that the one surviving original had been the only print made from the broken negative before it was discarded.

Pages 178 and 179: By first photographing Lincoln's son Tad on his pony, the photographer, Henry F. Warren, persuaded the boy to bring his father out onto the White House balcony, where these two poses and a lost third pose—possibly the last photographs of the living President—were made. Of one pose (see page 178), a few unretouched cartes-de-visite are all that remain. The second pose survives in the form of a few unretouched cartes-de-visite (see page 179) and numerous retouched contemporary albumen copy prints in several sizes. The surviving prints of both poses are vignetted. No original negative or contemporary copy negative of either pose is known to exist.

Page 180: This print was discovered in the archives of the Western Reserve Historical Society, in Cleveland, Ohio, in 1971 by the Lincoln authority Lloyd Ostendorf. Having recognized it as an unknown view of Lincoln at his second inauguration, Ostendorf published the picture for the first time in *Life* magazine in February 1972.

Page 189: On hearing of the two posthumous photographs of the President taken by Jeremiah Gurney, Jr., Mrs. Lincoln complained to Secretary of War Edwin Stanton, who immediately ordered General John Dix to seize and destroy the negatives and any prints. Dix confiscated both plates and destroyed one of them, along with its proof print, but he sent Stanton a small print from one frame of the second plate and asked that the multiple-image stereographic negative be spared. Stanton had this plate destroyed too, but he kept the print, which is reproduced. It was eventually given by Stanton's son to Lincoln's former secretary, John Nicolay, among whose papers, at the Illinois State Historical Library, it was found in 1952 by Ronald Rietveld, a fifteen-year-old student.

Page 193, lower left: Referring to this ambrotype, the artist's son, W. P. Brown, wrote to the Lincoln authority Ida Tarbell in 1896, "One of the ambrotypes I sold to the Historical Society of Boston, Massachusetts, and it is now in their possession." However, the compiler's efforts to locate the ambrotype have been unavailing.

Page 193, lower right: The only likeness known to have been made from the lost original negative of this pose is a single albumen print, heavily retouched with India ink. Though this print supposedly still belongs to the Smithsonian Institution and was seen there in the 1960s, the compiler's efforts to locate it have been unavailing.

It appears that Colonel William L. Bramhall asked Lincoln for his photograph after meeting him in New York City at the time of the latter's Cooper Institute appearance. "The photograph came even sooner than I expected," wrote Bramhall. "I determined to have struck at my own expense a campaign medal bearing the likeness of the party choice." This reference to the campaign medal, which was subsequently minted by George Lovett presumably from the Bramhall print, and the allusion to Lincoln's nomination for the presidency suggest that the sitting took place in Springfield, Illinois, during the spring of 1860.

Acknowledgments

The compiler wishes to express his lasting gratitude to Richard Benson, without whose superb craftsmanship these photographs could not have been reproduced with such a negligible loss of tone and definition. Of equal importance was the counsel of Marvin Israel, who insisted that only materials and processes of the highest quality be utilized in this book.

The Face of Lincoln could never have become a reality without the generous collaboration of Philip B. Kunhardt, Jr., who made the treasures of the voluminous Meserve Collection available for inclusion in these pages. And no less a vote of thanks is due to Lloyd Ostendorf, the foremost living authority on photographs of Lincoln, for having permitted the compiler to use twenty of the best likenesses in his collection and for having furnished a wealth of information about the histories of particular Lincoln photographs.

The masterly and elegant design which Gael Dillon gave to this book will surely be a source of delight to readers, as it was to the compiler. Likewise, the editor, Elisabeth Sifton, must be commended for her unfailing insight and consequent suggestions which radically altered, and substantially improved, the concept of the book.

James T. Hickey, of the Illinois State Historical Library, and Dr. Mark Neely, Jr., of the Lincoln National Life Foundation, were sources of counsel and pillars of support to the compiler during the years of research that this project entailed.

Nor was the government lacking in willingness to assist: Charles LaHood and Jerald Maddox moved mountains to make the very finest Lincoln material in the Library of Congress available to the compiler. Equal efforts in behalf of this book were made by Joe Thomas, Richard Conger, and Richard Youso at the National Archives, by David Haberstich at the Smithsonian Institution, and by Mike Harman of the National Park Service.

To Bryan and Chris Holme, Gage Cogswell, and Barbara Burn, among many others on the team at The Viking Press, the compiler wishes to express his profound thanks for work performed with diligence and expertise. He is also grateful to his friend Steven Aronson for some brilliant editorial work, and he wishes to compliment Carole Freddo on her superior copy editing.

Richard Cole and Charlee Brodsky performed wonders in their masterly repair work on some of the damaged photographs, and Sal Lopes also contributed much to the quality of many of the reproductions by his exquisite copy photography.

The curators and librarians to whom the compiler is indebted for research assistance include: Robert Dumas, of the Decatur (Illinois) Public Library; Stella Edwards, of the Reis Library at Allegheny College; Jay Monaghan, of the University of California; Weston Naef, of the Metropolitan Museum of Art; Kermit Pike, of the Western Reserve Historical Society; Robert Rosenthal, of the University of Chicago; John Stanley and Virginia Trescott, of the John Hay Library at Brown University; William Stapp, of the National Portrait Gallery; John Szarkowski, of the Museum of Modern Art; and John Tris, of the Chicago Historical Society.

The private owners, collectors, and dealers who either offered their photographs of Lincoln for publication in this book or assisted the compiler in his research activities include: James Ambrecht, Barbara Benoit, Maury Bromsen, Donald Gibson, Bruce Gimelson, Charles Hamilton, Carl Haverlin, John Hay, Harold Holzer, King Hostick, Laurence Ives, William Kaland, Manuel Keane, Lincoln Kirstein, Set Momjian, Beaumont Newhall, Ralph Newman, David O'Reilly, Milo Pearson, Jr., George Rinhart, Josephine Ross, Richard Stevenson II, Arthur Talansky, Samuel Wagstaff, Benjamin Weisinger, and Larry West.

The institutions not already mentioned which offered their photographs of Lincoln for inclusion in this book or made their research facilities available to the compiler include: Franklin and Marshall College, George Eastman House, the Henry Ford Museum, the Huntington Library, Knox College, Lincoln Memorial University, the Love Library at the University of Nebraska, the Mugar Memorial Library at Boston University, the Museum of Fine Arts (Boston), the New York Public Library, the Newark Public Library, the J. B. Speed Art Museum, the United States Army Military History Institute at the Carlisle Barracks, and the historical societies of the following states: Connecticut, Delaware, Illinois, Indiana, Iowa, Kansas, Maryland, Massachusetts, Michigan, Minnesota, Missouri, Nebraska, New Hampshire, New York, Ohio, Pennsylvania, Rhode Island, Vermont, Washington, and Wisconsin.

The book is set in Monotype Bell,
the earliest modern-style English typeface.
Bell type was designed by Richard Austin in 1788 for the British publisher and
educator John Bell, whose reforms entirely revolutionized the typography and format of newspapers.
The text was composed by Michael & Winifred Bixler, Boston, Massachusetts.